# WEIRD WISDOM

## AT WORK

# TRISH GOODFIELD

# WEIRD WISDOM

## AT WORK

First published in 2026 by Dean Publishing
PO Box 119
Mt. Macedon, Victoria, 3441
Australia
deanpublishing.com

Cataloguing-in-Publication Data
National Library of Australia
Title: Weird Wisdom at Work
ISBN: 978-1-764372-39-8
Category: Business/Diversity & Inclusion

The information contained in this book is provided for educational and informational purposes only. It is not intended as legal, financial, psychological, therapeutic, or professional advice.

While the author shares insights, experiences, and strategies related to business and relationships, every individual's circumstances are unique. Decisions regarding business ventures, partnerships, investments, or personal relationships should be made with careful consideration and, where appropriate, consultation with qualified professionals.

The author and publisher make no representations or warranties regarding the accuracy, completeness, or applicability of the contents of this book. They shall not be held liable for any loss, damage, or consequences arising directly or indirectly from the use or application of the information provided.

By reading this book, you acknowledge that you are responsible for your own decisions, actions, and results.

*To the few who tried to fit me into their boxes, and to the many who supported me to step outside of them. Your influence has shaped my Weird Wisdom.*

# CONTENTS

# "YOU'RE WEIRD"

Every big idea starts with a small, slightly awkward moment. Mine began with three words that stopped a meeting. And, as it turns out, started a movement.

When I was first told at work, "You're Weird," it wasn't delivered with malice, but it wasn't exactly a compliment either. The comment hung in the air, both unsettling and intriguing.

I had just asked a question in a team meeting. I thought I was being curious, but the reaction I got was a mix of raised eyebrows, awkward laughter, and that now-famous phrase: "You're Weird."

The meeting had been about a soon-to-be-implemented policy. While most of the team jumped straight into discussing the rollout details, I was more interested in stepping back and asking the bigger questions: How did we get here? What was the real purpose of the policy? What were we hoping to achieve, and were we addressing the root of the issue or just putting a bandaid on a single problem in one location?

I was the only one asking any questions, and I had lots of them. It was then that a colleague turned to me and said outright, "You're Weird."

Looking back, I realise my Weird Wisdom didn't

suddenly appear in that meeting room. It had been there all along, quietly doing its thing, often misunderstood, occasionally punished, and sometimes ignored. Like that moment in grade 2 when the teacher announced we were doing a test. I had no idea what a test was, so I did what any curious kid might do, I asked. I wasn't trying to be difficult. I wasn't being dramatic. I genuinely didn't know what a test was. The teacher responded, "Don't worry about that now, just answer the questions." Because I still didn't know what a test was, I simply didn't do it.

Years later, Mum told me the school had called her in. Apparently, my act of quiet refusal had caused a stir. Turns out, it was one of those IQ streaming tests, the kind schools use (and then often regret using) to sort kids into neat little boxes. My punishment? Being put in the same class as my twin brother for the rest of primary school. If you've ever had a twin, you'll understand why that felt like a cruel and unusual sentence. It was my first real lesson in systems and labels, how decisions made to enforce neat boxes rarely fit the people they affect.

Instead of throwing tantrums or lashing out, I retreated into observation mode. In fact, rebellion wasn't an option. It wasn't how our household worked.

My parents, especially Dad, were firm about how girls should behave and what was 'suitable' for us. I, on the other hand, quietly thought most of it was bollocks. I knew better than to say that out loud, though. Saying, "That's not fair" usually got me grounded for 6 weeks. And trust me, I tested it.

So instead of arguing, I tried a different approach. I started asking different questions, smarter ones. Instead of whining about fairness, I asked, "What do I need to demonstrate to be allowed to do this?"

.................................

*At 15, while I didn't realise it then,*
*I was already practising Weird Wisdom.*
*Working within the system while quietly*
*questioning it, finding another way through.*

.................................

The common thread in all these moments? I was always curious. Not just about the rules, but about where they came from. I wanted to understand the logic, not just follow the process. And when the logic didn't make sense, I didn't rebel; I redirected. I was always drawn to the gaps, the unspoken assumptions, the odd angles no one else was looking at. Not because I wanted to be contrary, but because I genuinely didn't understand why no one else seemed to see them.

All those years later when I was finally called Weird at work, it wasn't new – it was just named. While I'd felt different many times before, this was the first time someone had said it out loud. And strangely, it didn't sting. It landed with clarity, not confusion. I felt seen. Validated, even. It was as if someone had casually named the thing I'd always sensed made me, me. What struck me most wasn't the word itself, but how it made me pause and think: *Why did this label, often used to dismiss or belittle, feel so freeing?*

Maybe it's because, deep down, I'd always known I see and feel the world differently. I ask questions others don't. I make connections that don't follow a straight line. I spot the gaps in stories that others accept at face value. And while that way of thinking can make people uncomfortable, it's also where my strength lives.

..................................

*Being called Weird wasn't an insult. It was a kind of recognition. A quiet confirmation that I've never fit neatly into the boxes others expected me to. And for the first time, instead of trying to adjust or tone it down, I felt like owning it.*

..................................

It wasn't about being misunderstood. It was about remembering. Remembering the girl in grade 2 who didn't do the test because no one explained what a test was. The teenager who learnt quickly that saying, "That's not fair" would get her grounded for 6 weeks, but asking, "What do I need to demonstrate to be allowed to do this?" might just get her a step closer. That pattern – of thinking differently, questioning the rules, and navigating around them without making a fuss – had been there all along. I just didn't have the language for it.

That's what Weird Wisdom is. It's not something you pick up later in life like a skill or a strategy. It's something you remember. Something that was always there, a quiet undercurrent you may have ignored, hidden, or been told to suppress. But once it's named, once you recognise it, it becomes impossible to unsee, unfeel, or undo. It's not about being odd for the sake of it, or different to get attention. It's about seeing value in your own perspective, even if it doesn't line up with what's expected – *especially* if it doesn't.

That one moment, being called Weird, didn't change me. It reminded me. It gave me a language for something I'd always carried. Of course, I couldn't leave that mystery alone. My curiosity had already packed a bag and was halfway to the internet.

That evening, instead of brushing it off or stewing in self-doubt, I turned to Google. I wanted to understand why being 'Weird' didn't feel like an insult, but a badge of honour. What I discovered that night changed my perspective forever.

According to Oxford Languages, the word Weird has its roots in archaic Scottish English. There's also a reference to it in Norse mythology, which isn't surprising given the geographical proximity of the two regions and the Vikings' tendency to say, "We saw your light on and thought we'd pop over and invade you for a bit." It was originally spelled *wyrd*, and it didn't mean strange or odd back then. *Wyrd* referred to destiny.[1] A powerful concept that suggested each person has a unique path to walk. This wasn't about fitting in or following the crowd. It was about embracing what makes you singular, even if others don't immediately understand it.

. . . . . . . . . . . . . . . . . . . . . . . . . . .

*Wyrd, in its truest sense, was about owning who you are and recognising that your uniqueness is tied to your purpose.*

. . . . . . . . . . . . . . . . . . . . . . . . . . .

I sat with this revelation for a long time. It resonated deeply, almost like a confirmation. I realised that being called 'Weird' wasn't something to run away from; it was something to lean into. What if, instead of trying to fit in, I used my Weird as a strength? What if this so-called 'Weird' perspective was the very thing that could set me apart, drive innovation, and create meaningful connections? What if being 'Weird' was my wyrd? My destiny?

From that moment on, I stopped apologising for thinking differently. I stopped second-guessing my instincts and self-selecting out of conversations that needed a different perspective. Instead, I started recognising that the way I see the world has value, even if it doesn't always follow the usual path. I didn't need to explain it, defend it, or tone it down.

Rather than treating my difference as something to manage, I began to honour it. Not with fanfare or a need to stand out, but with a quiet confidence in how I see, sense, and shape the world around me.

And more importantly, I realised that Weird alone wasn't enough. It became clear to me that it's only Wisdom if you use it and share it. *What might happen if I use it intentionally, not just innately?*

This insight didn't just stay in my head; it transformed how I worked and led. I began to notice, really notice, how often workplaces celebrate conformity over creativity, uniformity over individuality.

As I was sitting with what it meant to really honour my Weird and use it well, I noticed a pattern. The idea of Weird kept showing up in different ways, particularly in conversations about how people work. That's when I stumbled across diversity of thought. I'd never heard the term before, so true to form, I went down a bit of a rabbit hole.

Around the same time, I was exchanging emails with Leon Coningham, head of the SBS Inclusion Program.

He explained that their inclusion work regularly speaks to innovation and diversity of thinking, but these are seen as outcomes of inclusion rather than something delivered as standalone training. As he put it, "We don't offer specific diversity of thought training. It's an outcome of being inclusive."

That didn't sit right with me. Having delivered training for years, I know there's no such thing as an 'automatic' outcome. People aren't plug-and-play. Growth doesn't work that way. More nuanced research moved away from the assumption that diversity of thought is an automatic outcome of DEI, and instead framed it as something that requires its own intention, attention, and practice, effectively positioning it as something that must be developed alongside DEI, not left to emerge on its own.[2] That felt much closer to what I was seeing and sensing. Interestingly, a few of the Weird Wisdom principles showed up in that research. Others didn't. But I didn't see that as a problem. If we all saw it the same way, well, that would kind of defeat the point, wouldn't it?

The systems and structures in many organisations are designed to reward predictability, but in doing so, they often stifle diversity of thought, the very thing that drives growth and engagement. I saw it happen around me all the time. People with unconventional ideas would hesitate to speak up, afraid of being labelled "too much," "out there," or "difficult." Teams would default to safe, familiar solutions that no longer worked instead of exploring bold, innovative approaches. And in the process, so much potential was left untapped.

I'm not an academic. I'm not a researcher either. But I will reference the work of others when it helps shine a light on these principles. And I'm sure there's research out there that would challenge what I've written. If you come across any, please share it. I mean it. As you'll see in Principle Three, I do love a good contradiction.

During my research, the more I read, the more I kept circling back to one thing: this isn't just theory. It's real, and it's showing up every day, in how people hold back, in how teams settle for safe, and in how much untapped insight quietly walks out the door. Several questions started bubbling up. How many people are hiding their Weird, because they've been conditioned to believe it's a flaw instead of a strength? How much collective Wisdom are we losing when people don't feel able to bring their best selves to work? And what's possible if we flip the script, if we encourage everyone to embrace their Weird and share their Wisdom?

This became the driving question of my career. It's what led me to develop the Principles of Weird Wisdom: five recurring ideas that showed up time and again in my work, in the people I coached, and in my own lived experience. These principles aren't just abstract concepts; they're deeply personal lessons I've learnt through embracing my *wyrd* and supporting others to do the same. Call it action-based research if it makes you feel better about the validity of these lessons. When I reflected on my Weird Wisdom, I noticed that the five principles improved how I worked and how the people around me worked too. They also helped us feel genuinely valued and more inclined to stay in our roles, even if our different approaches sometimes rubbed others the wrong way.

Before we jump into the principles, let's take a moment to define what a principle actually is. According to Oxford Languages, a principle is "a fundamental truth or proposition that serves as the foundation for a system of belief ..."[3] These five principles are just that: propositions, ideas to sit with, explore, and test for yourself. They're not rules, and they're certainly not linear or hierarchical. You'll likely find they overlap, influence each other, and show up in different ways depending on context. Please don't think of them as rules. They're tools. Flexible, powerful, and practical, tools for unlocking and honouring your Weird Wisdom.

The first principle is about being comfortable with the unknown. Embracing your Weird often means stepping into the unknown, taking risks, and challenging the status quo. It's not always easy, but it's where courage and insight start to meet.

The second principle is about seeing failure as growth. When you're willing to experiment and think differently, not everything will work, and that's okay. Every misstep is an opportunity to learn and evolve.

The third principle is about finding harmony in contradictions. Weird Wisdom often lives in the spaces where opposites collide. It's about holding seemingly conflicting ideas lightly and finding creative ways to integrate them.

The fourth principle is about challenging norms. Weird Wisdom isn't about being different for the sake of being different. It's about questioning assumptions and stretching boundaries to create something better.

And finally, the fifth principle is about exploring the unconventional. It's about giving yourself permission to imagine new possibilities. We'll do a deeper dive into each principle in chapter three and the chapters that follow.

Over the years, I've seen these principles transform individuals, teams, leaders, and entire organisations. When people feel empowered to embrace their Weird and share their Wisdom, amazing things happen. Satisfaction soars. Collaboration deepens. Inclusion becomes more than a DEI buzzword. It becomes a lived experience.

But it all starts with a choice. A choice to see your Weird not as a liability, but as an asset. A choice to use your unique perspective as a force for good. A choice to share your Wisdom with others, even when it feels vulnerable or risky to do so.

. . . . . . . . . . . . . . . . . . . . . . . . . . . . .

*So, if you've ever been told, "You're Weird,"*
*I invite you to see it as the highest compliment.*
*It's a sign that you have something valuable*
*to offer, something the world needs.*

. . . . . . . . . . . . . . . . . . . . . . . . . . . . .

Your Weird is your *wyrd*, your destiny. And when you embrace it, use it, and share it, you open the door to incredible possibilities.

This book is an invitation to explore that path. A nudge for anyone who's ever felt like they don't quite fit in. It's for individuals, leaders, teams, and organisations that want to build cultures where everyone's Weird is celebrated and everyone's Wisdom is valued, seeing real results in their bottom line. Because when we embrace our Weird and share our Wisdom, we don't just change ourselves; we change the way we work together.

And just so we're clear, this isn't a hero's journey. It's not an "I struggled, I overcame, follow me, and all will be wonderful" kind of story. Embracing your Weird is a work in progress, an ongoing evolution. Goodness knows the only principle I've nailed consistently is Principle Three. As your experiences grow, your Weird Wisdom grows with them. It shifts, expands, and keeps surprising you.

# THE WISDOM NOBODY TOLD YOU ABOUT

# THE CORE OF WEIRD WISDOM

Weird Wisdom is a way of thinking and being that values uniqueness, creativity, and the power of diverse perspectives. It's about recognising that your unique traits, your unconventional ideas, and even your failures aren't liabilities; they're assets. Weird Wisdom isn't just about being different for the sake of it; it's about using your individuality to contribute something meaningful, something no one else can offer.

At its core, Weird Wisdom is rooted in the belief that everyone has a unique destiny, or wyrd. But this destiny doesn't unfold on its own. It requires action, courage, and a willingness to share your insights and learn from others. Weird Wisdom reminds us that difference isn't a problem to solve; it's a strength to support.

..............................

*When people feel comfortable to show up
as they are, they're not burning energy
pretending or holding back. Teams get along
better; conflict becomes constructive instead
of personal, and organisations don't keep
bleeding time and money on recruitment,
because people actually want to stay.*

..............................

It's not about chasing big, flashy ideas. On the contrary, this often slows progress. Weird Wisdom is about creating space for real humans to do meaningful work together.

## MYTH–BUSTING WEIRD WISDOM

Before we dive deeper, let's bust a few myths about Weird Wisdom. These misconceptions often hold people back from fully embracing their Weird.

## Myth #1:
## Being Weird Means Being Unprofessional

There's a common belief that bringing your best self to work, differences and all, is somehow unprofessional. But professionalism isn't about fitting into a rigid preset standard; it's about showing up authentically and doing your best work. Weird Wisdom doesn't mean abandoning structure or disregarding norms entirely. It means finding ways to integrate your unique perspective into the professional world to add value.

## Myth #2:
## Weird Wisdom Is Inherently Disruptive

Another misconception is that being Weird is synonymous with being disruptive in a negative way. While challenging norms is a part of Weird Wisdom, it's not about creating chaos for the sake of it. It's about questioning assumptions and pushing boundaries in a way that drives progress. Weird Wisdom isn't an excuse to say what you want whenever you want and then brush it off with, "That's just the way I am."

## Myth #3:

## Only Certain People Can Be Weird

Weird isn't reserved for artists, tech geniuses, or other so-called 'creative types'. Everyone has a unique perspective to offer. Weird Wisdom is about tapping into that uniqueness, no matter your role, industry, or personality.

## Myth #4:

## Weird Wisdom Is Just Fluffy Feel-Good Talk

There's a perception that Weird Wisdom is too abstract or soft to be useful in the 'real world'. But it's actually the opposite. Weird Wisdom is a practical way to harness how people think differently, especially under pressure. It helps teams solve real problems using the most under-leveraged resource they already have: their people. Weird Wisdom starts with using the thinking you're already paying for. It turns unconventional insight into useful action. It's the stuff that doesn't fit the box, but ends up being exactly what the box needed.

## Myth #5:

## "I'm Not Weird, So This Isn't for Me"

Many people think Weird Wisdom only applies if you're quirky, loud, or visibly different. But Weird doesn't mean strange. It means uniquely you. It's your way of seeing, thinking, and solving that no one else does quite the same way. Weird isn't a label. It's your unique perspective that has been developed by your experiences and insights. Everyone notices things others don't. We approach certain problems and situations in different ways. That's what we build on.

## Myth #6:
## Weird Wisdom Is Too Playful to Be Taken Seriously

Playfulness is often mistaken for lack of depth. But Weird Wisdom balances lightness with insight. It uses humour and humanity to explore serious challenges without the eye rolls or burnout. Sometimes the most powerful conversations happen when we drop the jargon and speak like humans. Depth with levity is where trust and traction grow.

## Myth #7:
## This Isn't Relevant for the Corporate World

Actually, it's exactly where it's needed. In workplaces full of bland beigeness and systems fatigue, Weird Wisdom helps you use untapped potential, improve collaboration, and retain good people. It's not fluff; it's a practical approach that helps people at every level bring fresh thinking to how they work, connect, and contribute. It supports innovation, stronger teams, and healthier workplace cultures. The most forward-thinking organisations don't just tolerate difference – they use it. Weird Wisdom shows you how.

## Myth #8:

## This Is Just for Neurodivergent Folks

While neurodivergent thinkers often resonate with Weird Wisdom straight away, it's not a niche concept. It applies to anyone, whether you're highly analytical, deeply relational, structured, or spontaneous. It's about recognising how your thinking adds value, no matter your wiring.

## Myth #9:

## It's Just Another Diversity Buzzword

Weird Wisdom isn't about ticking boxes or making a poster. It's the practical application of diversity of thought. It's not enough to have different people in the room – you need to know how to make those differences work together. Weird Wisdom gives you the tools to do that. It's real-world, action-focused, and built to get better outcomes. Weird Wisdom is the hidden diversity.

**Myth #10:**
**It's Just for Personal Growth Junkies**

Yes, Weird Wisdom supports individual growth, but that's just the starting point. What makes it powerful is how it flows into team dynamics, leadership practice, and organisational culture, leading to hard results. It scales from self-awareness to systems thinking. It's not about self-help. It's about creating workplaces where people thrive and stay because they feel seen and useful.

## WHY WEIRD WISDOM MATTERS IN TODAY'S WORLD

Workplaces are facing complex, fast-moving challenges that don't have easy solutions. While there have always been complex issues, the pace has changed. The old ways of playing it safe, sticking to what has always been done, and avoiding discomfort don't work anymore.

..............................

*Weird Wisdom offers something different.
It values the unexpected insight, the
uncomfortable question, the person
who sees what others don't. This kind
of thinking helps people adapt quickly,
respond with clarity, and make decisions
that actually move things forward.*

..............................

When people feel they can bring their full thinking to the table, even when it's messy or unconventional, problem-solving sharpens; teams get stronger, and results speak for themselves. Weird Wisdom also makes space for healthy conflict. It doesn't avoid tension; it uses it. Disagreement becomes useful instead of personal. It opens doors instead of shutting them.

With so much focus on doing things fast and fitting in, Weird Wisdom invites something far more valuable: thoughtful disruption, honest collaboration, and the freedom to think differently.

## Innovation Requires Weird Wisdom

History's most remarkable leaps rarely come from those who play it safe or follow the rules without question. Instead, they come from people willing to ask the awkward questions others avoid, to ignore the safe well-worn path, and to trust their own unconventional instincts, even when those instincts feel Weird or risky. Whether it's the groundbreaking ideas of the past or the cutting-edge technology you rely on today, progress has always depended on individuals who challenge the status quo and disrupt the comfortable. These people are often met with scepticism, discomfort, or misunderstanding, sometimes for years. But it's precisely that willingness to stand apart and push boundaries that fuels innovation.

.........................

*Weird Wisdom isn't just a bonus or a quirky trait. It's essential. It's what fuels new ideas, shatters barriers, and drives the world forward. Without it, innovation stalls.*

.........................

## Diversity of Thought Drives Success

It's well established that teams made up of people with different backgrounds, experiences, and ways of thinking outperform those that all operate the same way. But diversity isn't only about who's in the room. It's about how people are encouraged to think, speak up, and contribute.

. . . . . . . . . . . . . . . . . . . . . . . . . . . . .

*Weird Wisdom puts value on the ideas that don't follow the script, the questions that slow things down for the right reasons, and the perspectives that make people stop and reconsider. It's not about always agreeing. Weird Wisdom is about creating space for tension, curiosity, and difference to shape better outcomes.*

. . . . . . . . . . . . . . . . . . . . . . . . . . . . .

When people are free to bring their full selves to their work – unpolished thoughts, unusual approaches, even productive disagreement – problem-solving improves, collaboration lifts, and teams stay engaged. Weird Wisdom doesn't just make work more interesting. It makes it more effective.

## Weird Wisdom Builds Resilience

Organisations succeed when they have people who don't just follow the script but are willing to bend it, question it, and rewrite it. Weird Wisdom encourages exactly that kind of thinking. It helps individuals tap into their creativity, adapt quickly, and see possibilities where others see roadblocks. Instead of fearing mistakes, it invites learning from them, turning mistakes into momentum. This approach pushes people to stay curious, stay flexible, and stay open to new ways of solving problems. It's about building confidence to explore unconventional ideas and resilience to keep going when the easy answers don't appear.

. . . . . . . . . . . . . . . . . . . . . . . . . . . . .

*When Weird Wisdom is embraced, teams become more resourceful and ready to face whatever challenges come their way. Not by avoiding difficulty, but by approaching it with a new perspective and a willingness to experiment.*

. . . . . . . . . . . . . . . . . . . . . . . . . . . . .

## WHERE WEIRD WISDOM SITS

Over the past few years, terms like thinking styles, cognitive diversity, psychological safety, and diversity of thought have made their way into workplace conversations. People sometimes hear about my work and say, "Ah, so you're talking about cognitive diversity" or, "This is about different thinking styles, right?" But Weird Wisdom sits in a different space, one that includes those concepts, but also stretches beyond them. This is how I differentiate the terms, but you may have others that work better for you.

**Thinking styles** describe how people prefer to process information and make decisions – whether someone is more analytical or intuitive, detail-focused or big-picture. These frameworks, like MBTI (Myers-Briggs Type Indicator) or HBDI (Herrmann Brain Dominance Instrument), are useful for understanding how people like to work, but they're based on preference, not challenge. They don't always push boundaries or spark the kinds of bold ideas that generate change. Weird Wisdom lives beyond those comfort zones.

**Cognitive diversity** looks at how people's brains actually function. This includes neurodiversity – such as ADHD, autism, and dyslexia – and the mental models people use to understand problems. It adds richness to teams, especially when tackling complex or unfamiliar challenges. But cognitive diversity is often invisible unless it's actively welcomed into the conversation. You can have a room full of diverse thinkers and still end up with groupthink if no one feels safe enough to say what they're really thinking.

**Psychological safety** – I tend to avoid terms like *psychological safety*. I'm not an expert in psychological safety, and to be honest, I think it has become overused, more of a buzzword for consultants, aspiring leaders, and speakers than a real driver of change. It gets thrown around, but little shifts in practice.

While most state legislation places responsibility for psychological safety squarely on leaders, Weird Wisdom takes a different approach. It's about *you*. Wherever you sit in a workplace, whatever your role, title, or task, you already have Weird Wisdom. It meets you where you are and encourages you to embrace your own Weird Wisdom and to guide and support others to embrace theirs too.

**Diversity of thought** takes it a step further. It's about what's actually expressed and shared. It shows up in the room when people challenge assumptions, offer different perspectives, and speak to what no one else has voiced. But even this relies on having the right conditions. Without cultural permission or individual courage, diversity of thought goes nowhere.

**Weird Wisdom** is the practice of ensuring our differences don't just exist – they get used. It brings together divergent thinking, life experience, emotional intelligence, and a willingness to challenge norms. It's not about who has the boldest ideas or the loudest voice. It's about whether those ideas are invited, heard, and allowed to shape outcomes. It doesn't require an organisational policy. It doesn't sit with leadership alone. It lives in day-to-day choices: to speak up, to stay curious, to invite difference.

Weird Wisdom asks: How can I, you, we create environments where what makes us different doesn't stay silent, but becomes the very thing that moves us forward? That's where the real shift happens.

## THE CALL TO EMBRACE YOUR WEIRD

If you've ever felt like you don't quite fit in, you're far from alone. Workplaces don't need another batch of people who think, act, and respond the same way. What they really need are more people willing to embrace their Weird – their unique way of seeing, thinking, and being – and to share that Wisdom boldly.

. . . . . . . . . . . . . . . . . . . . . . . . . . . . .

*Embracing your Weird isn't always comfortable or easy. It calls for courage to stand apart, vulnerability to show up as your full self, and the patience to navigate moments when you don't quite fit in.*

. . . . . . . . . . . . . . . . . . . . . . . . . . . . .

It might mean risking judgement or misunderstanding. But the rewards go far beyond personal satisfaction. When you let your Weird lead, you unlock possibilities, new ideas, and unexpected connections that can transform not only your own experience but also the groups and organisations you're part of.

# THE WEIRD EXCHANGE: GIVING AND GETTING WISDOM

# IT STARTS WITH YOU (BUT IT'S NOT ABOUT YOU)

Weird Wisdom isn't a one-way street. If you believe you possess Weird Wisdom, then you must also accept that everyone else does as well. Embracing your own Weird Wisdom opens the door to leveraging other people's unique gifts and helping them embrace their Weird Wisdom too. It's not about putting yourself on a pedestal; it's about recognising that we all have a Weird Wisdom, something special and unique that only we can bring to the table. When we tap into this uniqueness, both our own and that of others, extraordinary things can happen.

In one instance, I was tasked with conducting a diversity of thought review. I wasn't participating in this session; I was observing, quietly noting how ideas surfaced, how they were received, and where Weird Wisdom was being supported, or unintentionally shut down. Maya definitely wasn't the most extroverted person in the room. She didn't have seniority in title or tenure, and she didn't arrive with an air of knowing. What she had was a habit of asking questions that made people pause.

In this project meeting, the team was racing towards a solution everyone agreed was "good enough." Timelines were tight. The mood was decisive. Maya hesitated, then said, almost apologetically, "Can I ask something that might sound obvious?"

The room went quiet. That quiet where everyone stops thinking about what they're going to have for lunch. She asked one simple question about an assumption they'd all accepted weeks earlier. No challenge. No grand alternative. Just curiosity.

At first, the response was dismissal, as evidenced by protestations like, "We haven't got time to backtrack." But one colleague leant in. Then another. Within 10 minutes, the team realised they'd been solving the wrong problem. The plan didn't collapse in its entirety; it just needed a small adjustment. That early small adjustment saved months of rework later.

After the meeting, someone thanked Maya for speaking up. She shrugged it off. "I wasn't sure," she said. "I just needed to ask."

That was the exchange. She didn't need the right answer. She trusted the right question. Maya didn't position herself as the smartest person in the room. She trusted her Weird Wisdom enough to offer it, and the team trusted her enough to explore it. From then on, others followed suit. Questions came earlier.

Conversations got braver. Not because of a mandate, but because one person modelled that curiosity had value.

I wanted to cheer. I didn't. Well, maybe a little internally.

## THE RIPPLE EFFECT OF REALNESS

The beauty of Weird Wisdom lies in its reciprocity. When you own your individuality, you quietly invite others to do the same. It creates a ripple effect – one that goes far beyond creativity or teamwork.

In a work setting, when people genuinely value each other's strengths, perspectives, and ways of thinking, something deeper shifts: trust grows, pretence fades, and conversations become more honest. It changes the tone from cautious and surface-level to open and grounded. Weird Wisdom, when shared and embraced, doesn't just help teams work better – it helps people feel seen, stay longer, and contribute more fully without fear of being misunderstood.

When people feel they can share how they see the world, something powerful happens. Differences stop being barriers and start becoming building blocks.

...........................

*Weird Wisdom creates space for perspectives that don't always match, but often add value in unexpected ways. It strengthens resilience, leads to better decisions, and builds momentum – not by smoothing out the edges, but by making room for them.*

...........................

The mix of experiences, insights, and ways of thinking becomes the strength, not the challenge.

The power of this multi-way Weird Wisdom is in how it allows people to see and appreciate what they might otherwise overlook. We often focus on what's familiar or easy to understand, but it's the unconventional ideas, the different perspectives that lead to sustainable results. When you see others as having their own Weird Wisdom, you begin to approach them with curiosity and openness. You start to ask questions, to explore their ideas, and to consider possibilities that hadn't occurred to you before.

This approach is transformative for teams. It breaks down silos and fosters genuine collaboration. When people feel seen and valued for who they are, they're more willing to contribute, to take risks, and to support one another. Weird Wisdom becomes the glue that holds the team together, even in challenging times. It's no longer about individuals working in isolation; it's about collective Wisdom.

The benefits of embracing Weird Wisdom as a multi-way street reach into every corner of how people work and relate. When someone knows their perspective will be genuinely considered – not just tolerated – they're far more likely to speak up. That alone can change the quality of conversations, problem-solving, and decision-making. You get a broader view, not just a louder echo. But it doesn't stop there. When people feel that their input makes a difference, they tend to show up with more energy, care, and commitment. Morale lifts. Engagement deepens. People are more inclined to stay – not because they're told they're valued, but because they experience it in everyday interactions. Weird Wisdom helps create that kind of culture, where people don't have to filter out parts of themselves just to belong. Instead of chasing shiny new strategies, it's often this simple shift – genuinely valuing how people think – that becomes the game changer for long-term impact.

The teams within one organisation all had talent, experience, and the same problem: they kept talking past each other. Meetings were efficient but brittle. Decisions were made quickly, then revisited and raked over in corridors.

During a series of reset workshops, instead of pushing alignment, I asked them to do something uncomfortable: write down *how* they each thought, not *what* they thought. One team member wrote about coming from a frontline role where mistakes had immediate consequences. Another wrote about a background in strategy, trained to zoom out and challenge everything. A third admitted they processed ideas slowly and often needed time after meetings for processing. The writing was raw and unfiltered, something I rarely see when I ask people this question verbally. I could feel the energy in the room change. They stopped trying to 'correct' one another. The fast thinkers learnt to pause. The cautious ones were invited in earlier. The challenger wasn't labelled difficult anymore; they were asked, "What are we missing?"

The work didn't get easier. It got better. Tensions still surfaced, but earlier and with far less heat. Trust deepened because people no longer had to translate themselves to belong. The team didn't become the same. They became complementary. That's when Weird Wisdom turned from individual insight into collective strength.

## MORE THAN TICK-BOX DIVERSITY

As some workplaces pull back from traditional DEI efforts – often in response to political or public pressure – there's a risk of losing momentum on inclusion altogether. Weird Wisdom offers a different way forward. It challenges the narrow definitions of what 'qualified' or 'professional' looks like, which often exclude people who think differently, come from non-traditional backgrounds, or don't fit the usual mould. By recognising that everyone brings their own Weird Wisdom, organisations can go deeper than tick-box diversity. They can create space for genuine diversity of thought, where value is placed on how people see, sense, and solve things differently. This approach isn't about slogans or policies; it's about day-to-day actions that allow more people to contribute, belong, and thrive. And in times when inclusion is at risk of being deprioritised, that kind of practical, human-centred approach matters more than ever.

Weird Wisdom also encourages continuous learning

and growth. When you engage with other people's unique perspectives, you're exposed to new ideas and ways of thinking. This challenges your assumptions and expands your understanding of what's possible. It's a dynamic process that benefits everyone involved. As you help others embrace their Weird Wisdom, you're also refining your own. It's a feedback loop of mutual growth and discovery.

Think of a team like a mosaic made up of many different pieces, each with its own shape, colour, and texture. Alone, while each piece is interesting, when placed together thoughtfully, they create a picture far more striking and meaningful than any single piece on its own.

.................................

*Teams that practise two-way Weird Wisdom work like a mosaic. Each person brings their own unique perspective and strengths, and when those differences are respected and combined, the team becomes stronger, more adaptable, and better equipped to solve complex problems.*

.................................

Weird Wisdom isn't about blending everyone into one uniform shape; it's about fitting the pieces together so the full picture comes to life. That's how Weird Wisdom turns a group of individuals into a team capable of achieving results that none of them could manage alone.

Of course, embracing Weird Wisdom requires effort and intention. It's not always easy to see the value in perspectives that differ from our own. It's human nature to gravitate towards what's familiar and comfortable. Personal and professional growth kicks in when we stop staying safe and start engaging with the unfamiliar. This takes courage, empathy, and a willingness to be vulnerable. It's about creating space for others to shine, even when their approach or ideas challenge your own.

## EVERYDAY INFLUENCE

You don't have to be in a formal leadership role to influence your workplace. Using your Weird Wisdom – and encouraging others to use theirs – isn't the sole domain of managers or executives. In fact, it doesn't require any organisational decree at all. Influence happens at every level, whenever someone chooses to show up authentically and invite others to do the same. That's how tone shifts, and how real connection and collaboration begin.

Ultimately, Weird Wisdom is about recognising the value of individuality and leveraging it for collective success. It's about understanding that everyone has something unique to offer and that our differences are our strengths. By embracing your own Weird Wisdom and encouraging others to do the same, you create a ripple effect that transforms teams, organisations, and more.

So, the next time you find yourself working with a group of people, imagine them as pieces of a mosaic. Each piece has its own shape, colour, and texture – its own unique place in the bigger picture – waiting to be noticed and appreciated. Your role is to help each piece find where it fits best, to create a space where its individuality can shine and contribute to the whole. And in doing that, you'll discover that your own Weird Wisdom becomes even stronger and more meaningful. Together, these diverse pieces come together to form something far greater than any one piece alone: a picture that's richer, more vibrant, and truly remarkable. That's the beauty of two-way Weird Wisdom. It's not just about what you bring; it's about all of us, coming together to create something extraordinary through our differences and shared strengths.

..............................

*Ultimately, Weird Wisdom is about recognising the value of individuality and leveraging it for collective success. It's about understanding that everyone has something unique to offer and our differences are our strengths.*

..............................

By embracing your own Weird Wisdom and encouraging others to embrace theirs, you create a ripple effect that influences everything and everyone around you.

# UNLOCKING THE POWER OF WEIRD WISDOM THROUGH ITS FIVE PRINCIPLES

## VERSATILE TOOLS, NOT RIGID RULES

The ideas behind Weird Wisdom didn't appear out of nowhere. They grew from years of watching, experimenting, and reflecting. I noticed certain patterns in the way people really thrived when they leant into the unknowns, learnt from mistakes, challenged the usual ways of thinking, embraced contradictions, and asked questions others might avoid. Over time, these patterns became guiding ideas – tools meant to help, not to tell you what to do. Knowing how they came to life makes it easier to see them as flexible instruments for exploration, not rigid rules.

When we hear the word 'principle', it often makes us think of strict rules or non-negotiable standards. But in Weird Wisdom, these guiding ideas aren't absolutes; they're starting points. They give you a framework to explore, grow, and discover what works for you. They aren't fixed truths; they're tools to be questioned, tested, and shaped in your own way. They form the foundation of Weird Wisdom, an approach that encourages us to stretch beyond the usual, look at things differently, and make the most of diverse perspectives in work and in life.

It bears repeating – these principles aren't static truths but dynamic tools. The distinction between a proposition and a fundamental truth matters. After all, it would be more than a little ironic for someone advocating diversity of thought to insist there's only one right way.

The five principles of Weird Wisdom have been shaped and tested over many years, through real-world experience across sectors, cultures, and leadership styles. They've shown up in boardrooms, community meetings, coaching sessions, and conversations with people at every level of organisations, from those just starting out to those steering the ship. These principles reflect what happens when people stop hiding parts of themselves and start showing up fully, even when it feels risky.

Weird Wisdom can influence the way you do business, lead, follow, and collaborate. It shifts how you interact with teams, colleagues, clients, and communities. These principles help you navigate ambiguity, challenge the status quo, and connect more meaningfully with others. Over time, they build resilience, reduce conflict, and create a culture where inclusion isn't a checklist. Weird Wisdom helps people feel seen, valued, and able to thrive. Not despite their differences, but because of them.

The best part? Embracing Weird Wisdom doesn't require a job title or permission slip. Anyone can choose to embrace their Weird Wisdom at any time.

Let's delve into each principle to understand its significance and the benefits it offers.

## Principle 1: Being Comfortable with the Unknown

The unknown is part of being human. You know that feeling, the moment before you make a decision, try something new, or say something that matters. It's the space where you can't see the whole path ahead. Most of us have been taught to avoid it. We chase certainty, build plans, and hunt for the 'right' answers, thinking that if we can just control everything, we'll feel safe, capable, or in control.

But here's a truth: it's not a huge thing. Uncertainty isn't a monster; it's simply the absence of certainty. You don't need all the answers to keep moving.

Being comfortable with the unknown doesn't mean throwing away structure or wandering aimlessly. It means taking the next step even when the path isn't clear. Asking the awkward question. Trying something unfamiliar. Sitting with not knowing a little longer than what feels natural.

..............................

*The unknown isn't a problem if you don't let it be. It's the place where new ideas can grow.*

..............................

You've felt it before when you had an idea that went against the grain or something important to say but weren't sure how it would land. The unknown whispers, *What if I'm wrong? Misunderstood? Ignored?* That's exactly where Weird Wisdom starts to flex. When you act anyway, with curiosity instead of certainty, something shifts. You give yourself permission to be real, and in doing so, you make it easier for others to do the same.

In workplaces, the unknown and uncertainty are everywhere. They've always been present. It's the issues that are new, not the feelings. There have always been changing policies, economic pressures, social shifts, technological disruptions. There's often pressure to appear certain, to have quick answers, or to mask complexity with confidence.

Being comfortable with the unknown isn't about pretending you're fearless when challenges appear.

What's important is staying open, even when things don't make sense yet. It means trusting yourself enough to take a step without having all the answers. It invites a mindset that says, *I don't need to know everything to keep going.*

This principle sits at the heart of Weird Wisdom. If you can't sit with the unknown, you'll struggle to grow, adapt, or create anything truly different. Weird Wisdom thrives in that space, in the tension between what is and what could be. It asks you not to fight the unknown, but to sit with it, explore it, and even enjoy it.

When you stop needing certainty to feel secure, you open yourself to insight, connection, and progress that can't be planned, but can absolutely change you.

## Principle 2: Embrace Failure as Growth

Failure is one of the most misunderstood parts of being human. We're taught to avoid it at all costs, as if it's a sign of weakness, carelessness, or incompetence. Success is the goal; failure is a setback. But Weird Wisdom sees it differently.

. . . . . . . . . . . . . . . . . . . . . . . . . . .

*Failure isn't the opposite of success; it's
a necessary part of getting there.*

. . . . . . . . . . . . . . . . . . . . . . . . . . .

This principle invites you to reframe failure, not as a final verdict, but as a companion in the learning process. It's how you find out what doesn't work so you can move closer to what does. When you embrace failure as growth, you're less likely to give up, retreat, or stay silent. You're more likely to reflect, adjust, and keep going.

Failure shows up in many forms. It might be a conversation that didn't land the way you intended, a project that missed the mark, or a decision that led to unexpected consequences. Sometimes the hardest failures are the ones no one else sees: the risks you didn't take, the words you held back, the inner critic you couldn't silence. Weird Wisdom encourages you to look at these moments with compassion rather than criticism. What did you learn? What might you do differently next time? That's where growth lives.

In a group or workplace, how failure is treated sets the tone for everything else. If people are punished or shamed for making mistakes, they'll stop trying new things. They'll play small. But if mistakes are acknowledged openly, reflected on thoughtfully, and used as stepping stones, the culture shifts. People start taking ownership. They try bolder ideas. They support each other through missteps instead of pointing fingers.

If you're a Leader, whether titled or not, you have a big influence here. Talking honestly about your own failures and how you've grown from them gives others permission to do the same. They'll replace perfectionism with curiosity. They'll create space for questions like, *What did we learn?* and, *What might we try instead?* This kind of leadership isn't about pretending to have it all together. It's about showing that real progress often comes through trial, error, and a few faceplants along the way.

Outside of work, the same principle applies. In relationships, parenting, art, activism, wherever you care deeply, there's a risk of getting it wrong. But growth doesn't come from avoiding those risks. It comes from showing up anyway, learning through the stumble, and coming back with more insight and heart than before.

When you stop seeing failure as something to hide and instead see it as part of the creative, messy, courageous process of being human, everything opens up. You build resilience. You get better at adapting. And you learn to trust that even when things don't go to plan, you're still moving forward.

Failure isn't falling short. It's stepping into something new.

## Principle 3: Find Harmony in Contradiction

You grow up being told to pick a side, make a decision, or find the 'right' answer. You're taught to simplify things, label them good or bad, true or false, success or failure. But real life doesn't work like that. Most of the time, you're not operating in clear black or white but in a swirling mix of tones, textures, and contradictions.

. . . . . . . . . . . . . . . . . . . . . . . . . . . . .

*Life isn't just grey; it's filled with rich hues: the calm of blues, the heat of reds, the uncertainty of purples, and the vibrancy of yellows. Life is messy, dynamic, and often confusing.*

. . . . . . . . . . . . . . . . . . . . . . . . . . . . .

This principle invites you to stop trying to flatten or resolve contradictions and instead learn to live within them. Weird Wisdom encourages you to hold space for complexity not as problems to fix, but as realities to work with. Instead of striving for tidy answers, you can explore the questions more deeply.

In practice, this might look like accepting that two seemingly opposing things can be true at the same time. You can be confident and still have doubt. You can be a beginner and an expert in different areas. You can care deeply about someone and still need boundaries. Rather than tearing yourself in two trying to reconcile these contradictions, this principle asks: "What if the tension between them is where your real insight lives?"

In teams and workplaces, finding harmony in contradiction is an everyday challenge. You might be expected to deliver results quickly while also building long-term trust. You might need to honour the process while staying agile. You may be advocating for diversity while working in systems built for sameness. These aren't contradictions to be smoothed out; they're forces that can strengthen each other when held in balance.

As a leader, you may be expected to be both approachable and authoritative. At first glance, these can feel at odds, but when woven together with intention, they create in you a leader who's grounded and accessible. Likewise, in strategy, an organisation may face the tension between innovation and stability. Instead of swinging wildly between the two, leaders who embrace paradox learn to hold both values as essential. They make space for experimentation without losing their foundations.

This principle also shows up in community, relationships, and personal growth. You might want to speak up and stay safe. You might want to grow and stay grounded. You might feel joy and grief in the same moment. The goal isn't to eliminate the contradictions; it's to listen to them and let them shape something richer.

Finding harmony in contradictions doesn't mean you stop seeking clarity. It means you get better at sitting with uncertainty, holding more than one truth at a time, and seeing the full spectrum, not just the extremes. By learning to live with contradiction, you expand your capacity for empathy, creativity, and Wisdom. And you give yourself, and others, permission to be whole.

## Principle 4: Question the Norms

Norms are the invisible rules that shape how you think,

behave, and relate to others. They help create a sense of order, predictability, and shared understanding. But the very things that offer stability can also become barriers to growth if you never stop to question them.

Questioning norms isn't about being difficult or rebellious for its own sake. It's about pausing to ask, *Is this still serving me/us?* It invites us to look at long-held assumptions with different perspectives and consider whether they still make sense in the current context – personally, professionally, or as a society. Sometimes, the answer is yes. But other times, those norms are outdated, inefficient, or even harmful.

In the workplace, this principle can be transformative. Many of the systems and structures in organisations were created decades ago for a very different world. Whether it's how decisions are made, who gets heard in meetings, or how performance is measured, unexamined norms can limit inclusion, creativity, and impact. Challenging them creates space for more dynamic, responsive, and human-centred approaches.

For instance, consider how many businesses operate under the norm that productivity means being constantly busy or available. But does that really lead to better outcomes? Or does it drive burnout and disengagement? A leader who questions this norm might explore new ways of working that prioritise focus, well-being, and trust, ultimately leading to more sustainable performance.

Questioning norms can also be deeply personal. It asks you to look inward and notice the rules you've absorbed from society, family, culture, and past experiences. Perhaps you've been taught that success must look a certain way, or that your value is tied to constant achievement. Maybe you've internalised messages about what's acceptable to discuss, or who gets to take up space in a room.

..................................

*When you begin to notice your inherited beliefs,*
*you give yourself the chance to redefine them and*
*live in a way that feels more aligned and true.*

..................................

Of course, questioning norms isn't always comfortable. It can bring up resistance, from others, and from within yourself. It can stir up doubt, especially when you're stepping outside the familiar. But it also opens doors. It gives you room to experiment, to lead differently, to create systems that are more inclusive and effective, and to show up more fully as yourself.

It's also important to remember that norms are often maintained because no one has questioned them out loud. Sometimes all it takes is one person asking, "Why do we do it this way?" to spark a shift. And when that questioning comes with curiosity rather than judgement, it invites conversation rather than defensiveness.

Questioning norms helps you avoid getting stuck in autopilot. It invites you to be more intentional about how you live, work, and lead. When you regularly step back and examine the 'rules' you're following, both written and unwritten, you open up space for innovation, authenticity, and meaningful change.

## Principle 5: Explore the Unconventional

It's easy to stick to what you know. Familiarity offers comfort, and conventional Wisdom often feels like a safe bet. But safe doesn't always mean effective or fulfilling. This principle is about giving yourself permission to question the "way things have always been done" and imagine new possibilities. It's about being curious, courageous, and willing to venture into unfamiliar territory.

Exploring the unconventional doesn't mean rejecting everything traditional. It means looking at systems, processes, and assumptions with fresh perspectives. Sometimes you inherit ways of thinking or working without stopping to ask whether they still serve you. This principle encourages you to pause, reflect, and ask: *What else could be possible?*

In the workplace, exploring the unconventional might look like redesigning how meetings are held, how ideas are captured, or even how people are recognised and rewarded. It could involve letting go of rigid job descriptions in favour of more fluid roles that reflect people's strengths. It might mean building cross-functional teams that bring together unexpected combinations of skills and perspectives. These changes can feel disruptive at first, but they often lead to improvements in culture and performance.

Importantly, this principle isn't just about organisations. It applies just as much to how you show up individually. Exploring the unconventional means noticing your own habits of thought. Do you dismiss ideas too quickly because they seem 'too out there'? Do you assume something won't work just because you haven't seen it done before? Do you stifle your own voice because it doesn't sound like everyone else's?

There's also a personal courage that comes with this principle. It asks you to stretch, to say the thing no one else is saying, to try the method others think won't work, to back an idea that hasn't yet found its place. When you dare to step outside the lines, you not only create space for original ideas, but you also give others permission to do the same. This can be especially powerful in environments where conformity is expected or where people feel pressure to fit in.

Exploring the unconventional also honours the Wisdom that exists outside mainstream thinking. Whether it comes from lived experience, cultural traditions, grassroots communities, or unconventional career paths, there's rich insight in places that are often overlooked.

........................................

*When you're willing to be influenced by diverse perspectives and experiences, your thinking becomes more expansive, and your impact grows.*

........................................

It's worth remembering that almost every innovation we now take for granted began as someone's 'unrealistic' idea. Someone, somewhere was willing to challenge a norm, ask a better question, or take a different route. And the world changed because of it.

This principle isn't about being rebellious for the sake of it. It's about being honest enough to question, and brave enough to imagine more. Exploring the unconventional opens doors you didn't even know existed and invites you to walk through them with curiosity and intent.

## WHEN YOU PUT THE FIVE PRINCIPLES INTO PRACTICE ...

When applied consistently, these principles have the power to transform the way you lead, follow, and interact with others. They help you build more resilient, innovative, and inclusive organisations, and they enrich your personal lives by fostering growth, authenticity, and connection. By being comfortable with uncertainty and embracing failure, you develop the mental and emotional resilience needed to adapt to challenges and thrive in changing environments. Finding harmony in contradictions cultivates empathy and understanding, strengthening relationships and fostering collaboration. Exploring the unconventional and challenging norms creates a culture that values creativity, driving innovation and competitive advantage.

These principles provide a roadmap for inspiring and empowering people in workplaces. They help leaders navigate complexity, make bold decisions, and foster environments where everyone can contribute their unique strengths. For teams, these principles promote collaboration, innovation, and a climate where people feel able to speak up and try things. By embracing diversity of thought and creating space for experimentation, teams become more cohesive, dynamic, and effective. For individuals, these principles offer a path to personal growth and fulfillment. They challenge you to step out of your comfort zone, embrace your uniqueness, and approach life with curiosity and courage.

The five principles of Weird Wisdom – being comfortable with the unknown, embracing failure as growth, finding harmony within contradictions, exploring the unconventional, and questioning norms – aren't just propositions; they're invitations. They invite you to see the world differently, to think deeply, and to act boldly.

They challenge you to question your assumptions, expand your horizons, and unlock your full potential. Weird Wisdom isn't about fitting in; it's about stepping outside what's expected and discovering the extraordinary possibilities waiting there.

# DANCING WITH THE UNKNOWN (PRINCIPLE ONE)

## MEETING THE UNKNOWN

Change rarely waits for you to give it permission. It moves quietly through every part of your life: your relationships, your work, your plans, your identity. Sometimes it arrives gently, and other times it knocks the wind out of you. Either way, it's always there, reshaping what you thought you knew. Things are changing so quickly – technology, society, the economy – that uncertainty isn't a rare visitor anymore. It's always there, in the background. The question isn't how to avoid it, because you can't. The real question is: How do you meet it? Do you freeze and wait for clarity? Do you try to control every variable, hoping to feel safe again? Or can you take a breath, stay curious, and explore what might be possible even when you don't know what comes next?

Most of us were taught that the unknown is something to avoid. We plan, predict, and prepare so we can feel in control. We convince ourselves that certainty equals safety. Uncertainty isn't against you; it's just a natural part of being human. It's not a dark void waiting to swallow you. It's simply the absence of certainty. That space between what you know and what you don't is where creativity, courage, and growth live.

When we get comfortable with not knowing, everything shifts. Our attention moves from, *What if it goes wrong?* to, *What might be possible here?* That small change in perspective opens the door to new thinking, new conversations, and new solutions. You stop needing every answer before taking action. You start experimenting. You notice patterns, ideas, and insights that weren't visible before.

Weird Wisdom invites you to explore that space, not to rush through it. It's not about pretending uncertainty feels good. It often doesn't. It's about trusting that you can move through it without falling apart.

. . . . . . . . . . . . . . . . . . . . . . . . . . . . .

*Curiosity helps you see beyond the fear. Adaptability helps you respond to what's in front of you instead of clinging to what used to be. Openness allows others to join you in the exploration. Together, those qualities turn uncertainty from a barrier into a pathway.*

. . . . . . . . . . . . . . . . . . . . . . . . . . . . .

Think about the moments that shaped you most. They probably didn't happen when everything was neatly planned. They happened in the mess, the in-between, when things didn't go as expected. The promotion that didn't come through that pushed you to find something better. The project that failed but taught you what kind of leader you wanted to be. The time you didn't have a plan, so you had to make one up on the spot – and it worked. Those moments don't come from certainty. They come from stepping into the unknown and discovering what you're capable of.

The unknown isn't there to test you; it's there to teach you. It asks you to trust yourself, to stay curious, and to keep going even when the path isn't clear. Because when you stop fearing uncertainty, you start finding possibility. And that's where extraordinary things begin.

## WHY THE UNKNOWN MATTERS

Thriving in ambiguity isn't about taking reckless leaps or pretending to enjoy uncertainty. Cultivating a mindset that allows you to explore, test, and refine ideas, even when the next step isn't fully clear is key. Sometimes it's foggy; sometimes uneven, but if you keep moving, you start to see shapes, patterns, and possibilities emerge.

Curiosity is where it all begins. It's what nudges you to look closer, instead of shutting down, when something doesn't make sense. Curiosity says, "What's really happening here?" rather than, "This shouldn't be happening." It's not about having the right answers; it's about asking better questions. When you approach uncertainty with curiosity, you give yourself permission to wonder, to test, to play a little. You create room for questions that don't yet have answers – and that's where fresh thinking begins.

Adaptability works hand in hand with curiosity. Where curiosity invites you to explore the unknown, adaptability helps you adjust to what you find. You might discover that the idea you loved doesn't work in practice, or that a small, overlooked detail changes everything. Adaptability is the quiet skill of shifting gears without losing momentum. It lets you stay steady in the middle of change and confident enough to learn as you go. Imagine a workplace full of people who can do that.

The unknown isn't a hurdle to overcome; it's part of the creative process. Some of the most effective solutions emerge not from certainty, but from iteration. You try something; it half works; you adjust, and it gets better. Each step through the unknown gives you new data, new insight, and sometimes a completely different perspective on the problem you were trying to solve. Weird Wisdom thrives in that space. It doesn't demand perfection. It encourages movement – small steps, tested ideas, and lessons learnt along the way.

To begin, you don't need to have it all figured out. In fact, trying to get everything 'just right' before starting often means you'll never start at all. Think of ideas like tabletops floating in the air – full of potential, but needing legs to stand on. The legs might be people who bring complementary skills, time to develop the concept, resources to test it, or processes that give it shape. Some tabletops fall away; others get stronger. The point isn't to have every leg in place before you start; it's to trust that you can build as you go.

. . . . . . . . . . . . . . . . . . . . . . . . . . . .

*When you work with the unknown,
rather than against it, you open yourself
to more collaboration. You don't need to
use performative certainty or pretend
to know. You can say, "I'm not sure yet,
but let's explore." That single sentence
shifts the tone from one that fears
mistakes to one that values discovery.*

. . . . . . . . . . . . . . . . . . . . . . . . . . . .

When we embrace Weird Wisdom in workplaces, teams and ideas come alive. The unknown stops being something to fix and instead becomes something to learn from. Curiosity keeps you moving. Adaptability keeps you growing. Together, they turn uncertainty into progress, and that's where the real work of Weird Wisdom begins.

## HOW THE UNKNOWN SHOWS UP IN LIFE

Have you ever had a moment when an idea appears out of nowhere – mid-meeting, mid-conversation, or even mid-sentence? You start to share it, saying, "I've just had an idea …"

But before you've finished, someone jumps in with the practical questions: "How would it work? Who's involved? What will it cost?" Or worse, the three words that can stop momentum in its tracks: "Yes, but …"

And just like that, the spark fizzles. The room shifts from curiosity to control. The focus moves from what's possible to what could go wrong. It's a moment every team knows too well and a perfect example of how discomfort with the unknown can shut down exploration before it begins.

. . . . . . . . . . . . . . . . . . . . . . . . . . . . .

*Being comfortable with the unknown doesn't mean having all the answers. It means giving space for ideas to breathe before dissecting them. It means understanding that an idea isn't a plan.*

. . . . . . . . . . . . . . . . . . . . . . . . . . . . .

Weird Wisdom at work is about learning to sit in that moment of uncertainty and saying, "Let's see where this could lead" instead of rushing to decide if it's right or wrong. Ideas don't need to arrive fully formed. They grow through conversation, questions, and experimentation.

Now imagine that same meeting, but with a different tone. Someone shares an idea, and instead of interrogation, the group responds with curiosity: "That's interesting, tell us more." Or, "What if we explored it a bit?" That simple shift in language changes the whole dynamic. Suddenly, the idea isn't a problem to solve but a possibility to explore.

Once you recognise that ideas don't need to be fully formed to have value, the next step is noticing how much we try to control the path forward. We instinctively want to map every step, plan every outcome, and manage every variable so nothing unexpected happens. But here's the catch: that grip on certainty often limits the very creativity and discovery you're trying to unleash. The act of holding too tightly can blind you to new possibilities, shut down experimentation, and make the unknown feel like a threat rather than a doorway.

# THE ILLUSION OF CONTROL

Understanding the illusion of control is essential. Letting go doesn't mean chaos takes over; it means giving yourself and others the space to respond, adapt, and explore. It's a mindset shift that allows curiosity and flexibility, instead of rigid plans or the fear of making a mistake, to guide action.

Most of us crave control because it feels safe. We tell ourselves that if we can plan every step, anticipate every outcome, and manage every variable, we can avoid mistakes, disappointment, or chaos. But control is mostly an illusion. Life is complex, messy, and unpredictable. No matter how tightly you grip the wheel, there will always be forces beyond your influence.

The trick isn't to eliminate uncertainty; it's to loosen your grip enough to notice it, respond to it, and even welcome it. When you stop trying to force outcomes, you start seeing possibilities that rigid plans would have obscured. You can pivot, adapt, and act with curiosity instead of fear. You don't have to have all the answers to move forward. What matters is your willingness to explore, test, and adjust.

Expect some resistance along the way. When you show comfort in the unknown, people around you might push back. They may worry about looking foolish, feel the need to protect the group from chaos, or simply crave closure. None of that means your curiosity or willingness to explore is wrong. Leaning into uncertainty isn't reckless. On the contrary, it's where growth, insight, and better solutions begin.

.................................

*When you allow yourself to loosen control, the unknown stops feeling threatening. It becomes a space where ideas can take shape, experiments can unfold, and creativity can thrive.*

.................................

In Weird Wisdom terms, it's not about being fearless; it's about acting with courage despite fear. That courage is contagious. When you model comfort with uncertainty, others are more likely to lean in, share ideas, and take their own small leaps into the unknown.

I was brought in to work with a mid-sized engineering firm of 230 employees after their employee engagement survey highlighted a common theme: uncertainty was stressful, and many people felt hesitant to speak up or try new approaches. Previous leadership styles had left employees acting cautious. Project managers stalled early prototypes until every risk was mapped. Engineers hesitated to test new materials. Operations and support staff held back workflow ideas. The unknown felt unsafe, and innovation was stifled.

Over the course of a year, we shifted the focus from rules to mindset. Leaders modelled curiosity, openly acknowledging what they didn't know and inviting ideas from everyone. Their approach was contagious. Small, safe experiments became the norm: engineers trialled alternative materials on low-risk components; project managers tested iterative scheduling, and support staff piloted new reporting approaches.

Slowly, the workplace culture began to change. Uncertainty became a space for exploration rather than fear. Teams embraced feedback, tested ideas, and collaborated across roles in ways they hadn't before. By year's end, engagement scores had improved by 18 percent; project timelines shortened by an average of 12 percent, and the number of new process or product ideas implemented doubled.

The unknown was no longer a barrier; it had become a playground for growth, creativity, and collective problem-solving. Employees felt empowered to contribute ideas without fear of judgement, and the organisation as a whole became more adaptable, resilient, and curious.

When teams lean into the unknown together, something powerful happens. They move from a culture of caution to one of curiosity. They begin to see that uncertainty isn't chaos – it's potential. That's where creativity lives. When people feel comfortable to explore half-formed ideas without fear of judgement, they open the door to unexpected insights, better questions, and more innovative outcomes.

The unknown also shows up in smaller, everyday ways. It's in the pause before you speak up with a new perspective. It's in the decision to take on a project that stretches you beyond your current comfort zone. It's in those moments when you don't yet know what success looks like, but you show up anyway. Each time you do, you strengthen your capacity to navigate ambiguity with confidence.

If you're a leader, you play a big part in how teams handle those moments. As a leader who models curiosity – who says, "I don't know yet, but let's explore it together" – you signal that it's okay to not have all the answers. You show that discovery is part of the process, not a detour. Over time, that kind of leadership builds a culture where people are more likely to share new ideas, challenge assumptions, and take thoughtful risks.

## LIVING WITH THE UNKNOWN

The unknown isn't an empty space to be feared. It's where life and work actually happen. Growth, creativity, and insight all live there. When everything feels certain, you're usually just repeating what you already know. It's only when you step into the uncertain – when you don't yet know how things will turn out – that something new can take shape. That's where innovation is born, where learning deepens, and where you begin to surprise yourself.

Getting comfortable with the unknown isn't about pretending to enjoy chaos. It's about staying steady when clarity hasn't arrived and trusting yourself to move forward, even when the full picture isn't clear yet. This is where resilience begins, not in having all the answers, but in trusting your ability to keep learning as you go. Each time you navigate the unknown, you strengthen the muscles of adaptability and curiosity. And curiosity really is the key.

..................................

*When you don't rush to fill every gap with an answer, you create space for better questions. You start wondering, **What else could this mean? Who else might see it differently?** That curiosity opens doors to diverse perspectives.*

..................................

When you stop pretending to know it all, you naturally invite others in. You ask; you listen; you discover how someone else's experience or insight can stretch your own. That's how collective Wisdom grows. Not from certainty, but from the willingness to explore together.

The unknown also invites a different kind of learning. The kind that comes from testing, observing, and adjusting. You don't need to wait for perfect information or a flawless plan. Small experiments, done with intention, create movement. You try; you gather feedback; you adapt. That's action-based learning – the art of shaping ideas through experience rather than theory. It's how innovation actually happens: one thoughtful experiment at a time.

Of course, all of this takes courage. Stepping into the unknown never feels entirely safe. You'll have moments of doubt, fear, or second-guessing. To speak up, to test an idea, to ask a question that might not have an easy answer takes courage. And the thing about courage is it spreads. When someone sees you take that step, it gives them permission to do the same. Before long, courage becomes part of how your workplace operates.

Here's what's worth remembering:

- ◆ The unknown is natural and human. You're never meant to have all the answers. None of us are.
- ◆ Uncertainty isn't something to fear. It's a space to create. It's where ideas, creativity, and new discoveries take shape.
- ◆ Growth lives in the tension between what is and what could be. That tension can feel uncomfortable, but it's also the heartbeat of progress.
- ◆ Your response is always a choice. You can shrink back, wait for certainty, and play it safe. Or you can lean in with curiosity, explore, and see what might emerge.

◆ Most importantly, small steps matter. You
   don't need a grand plan or total confidence.
   Experiment, learn, adjust, repeat. That's how real
   transformation happens.

When you start to see uncertainty as part of the process and not a sign that something's gone wrong, things start to change. You become less reactive and more responsive. You stop waiting for the perfect conditions and start creating them. You realise that the unknown isn't working against you; it's working with you.

Weird Wisdom reminds us that being comfortable with the unknown isn't about having no fear; it's about trusting yourself and others to find your way through. The unknown is where life stretches you, surprises you, and shapes you. It's where possibility lives. And each time you choose to stay curious instead of certain, to act instead of avoid, you build a deeper kind of confidence – one rooted not in control, but in courage.

That's where Weird Wisdom truly comes alive: not in knowing, but in exploring what's still to be discovered.

## IDEAS TO SIT WITH

1. **The unknown isn't the enemy** – it's where creativity, growth, and new insight begin.

2. **Certainty isn't safety** – learning to move forward without all the answers builds resilience and adaptability.

3. **Curiosity opens doors** – when you don't rush to know, you make space for diverse perspectives and shared Wisdom.

4. **Progress is experimental** – small steps, reflection, and adjustment instead of rigid plans lead to stronger outcomes.

5. **Courage is contagious** – acting despite uncertainty gives others permission to do the same.

# THE ART OF GETTING IT WRONG
## (PRINCIPLE TWO)

## REDEFINING FAILURE

You know that moment when your stomach drops – the instant you realise something's gone wrong? Maybe you sent the wrong report, missed a detail, or made some other critical mistake. The mix of embarrassment, frustration, and self-doubt hits hard. It's uncomfortable, and for a moment, you want to disappear or fix it before anyone notices.

Failure is part of working life. It's inevitable. No matter your role, experience, or good intentions, things sometimes go wrong. A project might not meet its goals; a client conversation might go sideways, or a new idea you championed might flop. That's not a reflection of your worth or ability; it's simply part of how work happens. Yet for most of us, failure triggers a physical reaction: tension, discomfort, and a need to retreat. That sinking feeling when something doesn't go as planned – it's deeply human.

The problem is that workplaces often treat failure as taboo. You see it in the quick defensiveness in meetings, in the silent passing over of ideas that might not work, and in the undercurrent of blame when mistakes surface.

..........................

*When failure becomes something to hide
or fear, you stop taking risks. You stop
speaking up. You stop trying new approaches.
Creativity stalls, confidence erodes, and
ideas never get the chance to grow.*

..........................

I was working as a contractor with a national organisation long before I fully understood the value of my own Weird Wisdom. The company was attempting to restructure a department, yet the entire organisation was entrenched in a blame culture. Mistakes weren't learning opportunities; they were public spectacles, and people were fired on the spot, often in front of colleagues. Staff kept their heads down, especially whenever someone from head office was onsite.

Amid this environment, another department identified a potential cost-saving measure: switching from physical textbooks to ebooks, which could save hundreds of thousands annually. One lone voice urged caution, but their concerns were drowned out by the seniority and authority of others in the working party. Ultimately, the most senior person made the final decision, and a $150,000 purchase order was processed.

During the dissenting employee's holiday, decisions were effectively made in their absence. Upon returning, they were blamed for authorising an unbudgeted expense. Senior colleagues remained silent. Luckily, this employee had printed copies of the emails showing the decision-making process, proving they weren't at fault. They kept their job, but the incident highlighted a painful truth: the organisation had no appetite to learn. The blame culture persisted, stifling collaboration, silencing voices, and ultimately contributing to the organisation's decline.

I was only involved in this story as a spectator, but I learnt a key lesson: when individual Weird Wisdom is ignored, silenced, or punished, the cost is both human and financial. Valuable insights are lost; trust erodes, and decisions that could have been smarter and less costly are compromised.

Reframing failure changes all that. Instead of a verdict on your competence, failure becomes feedback. It becomes insight. It becomes an opportunity to see what's working, what's not, and how you might do things differently next time. Failure isn't just about the things that go wrong; it's about learning, adapting, and growing.

You can start by redefining what counts as failure. Don't limit it to catastrophic outcomes or blown deadlines. Expand it to include mistakes, missteps, and miscalculations. Every misstep has a story to tell. Every miscalculation teaches something. They all contain lessons that you won't get anywhere else. When you look at your work through this perspective, the unknown, the missteps, the things that make you uneasy, stop being threats. They become opportunities to experiment and to stretch yourself in ways that only trying (and sometimes failing) can teach.

When you embrace this mindset, you change your relationship with risk. You stop fearing that each decision might define you. Instead, you begin to see each outcome as data, as information that guides your next move. You become someone who can step into uncertainty with curiosity rather than anxiety. You start to ask questions like, *What did this teach me?* or, *How can I use this insight next time?* rather than, *Who's going to blame me for this?*

The key is perspective. Failure isn't a verdict on your ability. It's the raw material for growth. It's the place where insight lives, where innovation sparks, and where resilience is forged. By reframing failure, you reclaim the power to learn from every experience, to take action despite uncertainty, and to keep moving forward. Your mistakes are no longer just errors; they're stepping stones on the path to better ideas, stronger solutions, and a more confident, capable you.

## THE COST OF BLAME CULTURE

You've probably been in a workplace where the first reaction to a mistake is to find someone to blame. Maybe it was a miscalculated budget, a delayed project, or a client complaint. You know the drill: fingers point, excuses fly, and the room fills with tension. When blame dominates, it doesn't just affect the person singled out. It ripples through everyone around them, including you.

If you're constantly walking on eggshells, thinking twice before speaking up or testing a new idea, you're living in a blame culture. You hold back; you avoid taking risks, and you start second-guessing yourself. Even small errors feel dangerous. Creativity slows; people leave, and the energy that could drive your team forward gets trapped in fear.

Blame culture also has very real consequences for you personally. You may take on undue guilt for things that weren't fully in your control, or replay mistakes in your mind long after the meeting ends. That stress builds up. Your confidence dips. You stop volunteering for challenging projects. Over time, your engagement at work can drop, and you may start to question whether your ideas, or even your presence, are valued.

And it's not just you. When your whole organisation operates this way, the cost multiplies. Decisions get delayed because everyone is waiting for the 'perfect' plan. Teams become risk-averse. People hide mistakes rather than sharing them, which means learning is lost. Ideas dry up. The organisation becomes less agile, less competitive, and more likely to repeat the same errors.

You can step out of this cycle. Shifting your perspective and helping influence others to do the same starts with seeing failure differently. Instead of asking, "Who messed up?" start asking, "What can we learn?" Instead of hiding your own mistakes, try sharing them in a constructive way, highlighting what insight you gained. That's how you model a different approach.

Post-mortems are your friend here. They aren't about blame; they're about understanding. After a project, take a moment, on your own or with your team, to explore what worked, what didn't, and what could improve next time. Ask questions, dig into the details, and seek perspectives from people who weren't directly involved. This isn't just a process; it's a mindset. It trains you to see failure as a source of insight, not a reason for judgement.

When you embrace this mindset consistently, something changes. You notice that your stress around mistakes eases. You feel more confident to share ideas, experiment, and test solutions, even when the outcome isn't guaranteed.

Others around you take notice, and slowly the tone changes. The room becomes safer, not because someone waved a magic wand, but because people like you began responding to failure with curiosity, not fear.

. . . . . . . . . . . . . . . . . . . . . . . . . . . . .

*Blame culture comes at a cost: your confidence, your energy, and your ability to grow. But by seeing failure as a source of insight and learning, you reclaim that space.*

. . . . . . . . . . . . . . . . . . . . . . . . . . . . .

You don't just survive mistakes; you use them to become better, bolder, and more resilient. The next time something goes wrong, remember – it isn't the end. It's the start of growth, and you get to decide how you respond.

## SEEING FAILURE AS OPPORTUNITY

It's easy to view failure as a stop sign, a signal that something went wrong and you should retreat. But what if you started seeing failure differently, as data rather than a setback? Every misstep carries valuable lessons that can guide you towards better decisions, smarter strategies, and more creative solutions. When something doesn't go as planned, it isn't the end of the road; it's an invitation to pause, reflect, and adjust.

Shifting your mindset in this way isn't about pretending mistakes don't matter. On the contrary, it requires paying attention to what happened, analysing why it happened, and asking questions like: What can I learn here? What assumptions were off? What might I do differently next time? Each failure holds clues – sometimes subtle, sometimes obvious – that can inform your next move.

One of the most powerful perspectives is recognising that not everything in a failed initiative is broken. Often, parts of the work were solid – ideas, processes, or approaches that worked well but didn't align perfectly with the outcome. These 'salvageable pieces' can stand alone, or be repurposed or recombined with new approaches to create something even better. A failed project isn't a total loss; it's a toolkit of insights, some ready to use immediately, others to inspire future experiments. Learning to separate what worked from what didn't turns failure into a source of innovation rather than discouragement.

Mark Kable, CEO and managing director of Harvest Moon, was overseas at an agricultural convention – an event that showcases different crop varieties from across regions. Among all the produce on show, one type of carrot caught his eye. It was "nearly in the bin," stunted, and maxing out at just 11 cm long. The breeder was ready to discontinue the variety, seeing only failure. Out of everyone present, Mark was the only one who saw potential. He began wondering: *How could this rejected carrot become the snackable carrot of the future?*

What followed was far from an overnight success. The first 4 years were filled with trials, experimentation, and setbacks as the team worked to turn a stunted carrot into a commercially viable product. Growing, harvesting, and selecting the right carrots involved repeated 'failures'. But each misstep offered valuable lessons, revealing what worked, what didn't, and what adjustments were needed for the next attempt.

The experimentation didn't stop with the carrot itself. Packaging, distribution, and shelf placement were all tested and refined. Each failure was treated not as a verdict, but as feedback. Over 9 years of persistence, these small experiments gradually coalesced into success. The team identified the optimal carrot traits, perfected packaging, and positioned the product for consumer appeal.

Eventually, snackable carrots became a commercial hit, delighting consumers and creating a new category in the market. What was once considered a failed carrot became an iconic snack — all because someone was willing to see opportunity in what others dismissed.

The key lesson from Harvest Moon's journey is that failure isn't the end point; it's part of the process. Without the 'failed' carrot, I wouldn't be enjoying a snackable carrot as I type. Every misstep provided information that guided the next step, across product development, packaging, and distribution. Embracing failure, staying curious, and experimenting deliberately transformed a rejected carrot into a breakthrough product.

The Harvest Moon story isn't just about carrots; it's about perspective. Failure isn't the end; it's information. The missteps, the 'almosts', the awkward experiments were all part of the journey. Think about your own work. How often have you dismissed an idea, project, or process because it didn't look perfect at first? Harvest Moon's story reminds you that every 'failed carrot' has lessons, hidden potential, or pieces that can be recombined into something remarkable.

. . . . . . . . . . . . . . . . . . . . . . . . . . . . .

*By staying curious, experimenting thoughtfully, and learning from what doesn't work, you can transform setbacks into breakthroughs.*

. . . . . . . . . . . . . . . . . . . . . . . . . . . . .

Failure also comes with emotions. Disappointment, frustration, embarrassment, even shame. All these feelings are natural. You're human, and work matters to you. But acknowledging these emotions doesn't weaken you; it gives you clarity to respond intentionally rather than react out of fear or defensiveness. Reflection, alone or with supportive colleagues, helps you process what happened, extract insights, and regain confidence. Sharing experiences with others can normalise the experience and foster collective learning.

When you start seeing failures as opportunities, the way you approach your work changes. You become willing to test new ideas, take measured risks, and explore unconventional solutions. Over time, what was once seen as risky or unsafe becomes part of a culture of learning, innovation, and resilience.

My first permanent management role started off brilliantly, or so it seemed. I had one staff member who was a rockstar. The truth is, though, I wasn't really a leader yet. I was barely a manager. Sure, I was responsible for the centre and its tasks, but my day-to-day work wasn't much different from what I'd been doing before: direct care.

Then, over a Christmas break, the organisation merged two services into one and made me the manager of both. Suddenly, I went from one happy, engaged staff member to eight – seven of whom were angry that 'their' manager hadn't been given the job. I was completely unprepared to navigate this level of distrust and received no support. Everything still got done, but we were all miserable. I felt like I'd made a huge mistake accepting the role. The self-recrimination was paralysing.

After 16 months, I moved into a new role – still leadership, but without direct staff management. My confidence had been shaken, and I wasn't in a hurry to repeat the experience. But I used that time to reflect, giving myself grace space to learn and apply what I had learnt. I tested different approaches, sought perspectives, and considered how I might have done things differently.

When it was time to lead again, I took a different approach. I ditched the "I've got this" rhetoric I'd been programmed to adopt and led with "I'm not sure." I continued to make mistakes, but they no longer paralysed me. I learnt from them, sought clarity, gave myself grace space, and then started over, again and again.

That's perseverance in action – not blind persistence, but the quiet discipline to keep showing up and to try again with new insight. Perseverance isn't about pushing through at all costs; it's about staying curious enough to keep learning. Each small adjustment builds momentum, and over time, that momentum becomes confidence

Failure is inevitable. But it doesn't have to be negative. By embracing failure as opportunity and recognising the value in what worked, you give yourself permission to learn, adapt, and move forward with confidence. Each misstep isn't a defeat – it's a stepping stone on your path to growth, creativity, and meaningful contribution.

## FROM STUMBLE TO STRATEGY

When you start seeing failure differently, the changes are noticeable – both for you personally and for the people you work with. On your own, embracing failure gives you confidence. You start to step into challenges, knowing that mistakes aren't the end of the world. They're just part of figuring things out. Along with confidence comes adaptability. Every misstep teaches you how to adjust, pivot, and respond differently next time. You become more resilient, bouncing back from setbacks instead of letting them stop you. And just as important, you develop self-compassion. You stop beating yourself up for getting it wrong and start treating errors as part of being human. That small shift alone, giving yourself grace space to reflect rather than react, builds enormous capacity for growth.

As you do this, curiosity naturally follows. Instead of replaying mistakes privately, you start asking questions out loud: "What did I learn from that? What might I try differently next time?" These conversations are small signs that failure is starting to be seen as feedback, not fault. Teams that reach this point begin to show real Weird Wisdom maturity. They're learning to treat every setback as information.

When your team embraces this mindset, the energy lifts. People talk openly about what worked *and* what didn't without fear of blame. A post-project conversation becomes less about "who got it wrong?" and more about "what could we reuse next time?" That's when you know you're moving from friction to traction. The space becomes safer for sharing ideas, even the ones that might flop. Teams start experimenting, testing, and adjusting as they go. You might see it in the team that revisits a project that once fell flat, trying again with fresh insight instead of shelving it for good. Collective perseverance is about staying with the work long enough to uncover what's possible, even when the first few tries don't deliver. Every misstep becomes a data point, and the language of 'failure' starts to sound more like 'iteration'.

When Weird Wisdom is at work, you'll see people

running small experiments and talking about learning, not losing. But when it's not, silence fills the room. People hold back, avoid risk, or quietly replay mistakes on their own instead of reflecting together. That's when perfectionism and fear still have a foothold. The turning point comes when someone models curiosity instead of control. When someone shares their own misstep and what they learnt, it signals that reflection is valued more than perfection.

At the organisational level, this shift is profound. When mistakes stop being treated as verdicts, the whole system becomes more agile. Decisions get made faster because people aren't waiting for perfect data. Teams experiment with confidence because they know learning is valued, not punished. Engagement improves because people feel trusted and supported, not judged. Retention rises as staff realise their contributions matter, even when outcomes don't land perfectly. Innovation thrives because ideas aren't dismissed at the first sign of imperfection. They're tested, refined, and tried again.

You'll also notice cultural indicators of this shift: conversations move from "who failed?" to "what did we learn?"; people reference 'grace space' as something real, not fluffy, and innovation often comes from recombining things that once didn't work. It's the Harvest Moon mindset – every 'failed carrot' has potential if you stay curious enough to look.

Ultimately, failure starts to redefine what success looks like. It's no longer about flawless execution or avoiding mistakes. You're seeing progress, reflection, and growth.

. . . . . . . . . . . . . . . . . . . . . . . . . . . . .

*Each misstep becomes a stepping stone,*
*each hiccup a lesson, and each challenge*
*an opportunity to stretch further.*

. . . . . . . . . . . . . . . . . . . . . . . . . . . . .

You, and everyone around you, begin to see that setbacks aren't endings. They're invitations to experiment again, learn again, and lead again with a little more Weird Wisdom each time. The next time something doesn't land the way you'd hoped, pause before you retreat. Ask yourself what part of it worked, what you learnt, and how you'll try again. That reflection, that willingness to stay in the discomfort a little longer, is where growth actually begins.

## IDEAS TO SIT WITH

1. **Failure isn't final; it's data.** Every misstep tells you something important if you take the time to listen.
2. **Mistakes are messy but necessary.** Growth rarely comes from smooth, predictable paths.
3. **Curiosity trumps blame.** Ask, "What can I learn?" instead of, "Who's at fault?"
4. **Failure shapes resilience.** The more you fail thoughtfully, the stronger and wiser you become.
5. **Share your stories.** Opening up about your stumbles invites others to learn, take risks, and innovate alongside you.

# TWO, OR MORE, TRUTHS CAN TANGO (PRINCIPLE THREE)

# THE BEAUTY IN THE TENSION

This one's my favourite principle. Maybe because I see so much of myself in it. In my speaker bio, I describe myself as a colourful mix of contradictions, balancing caution and courage, playfulness and seriousness, idealism and practicality. Those words aren't just for show; they reflect how I move through life and work. Some days, I'm charging ahead with bold ideas. Other days, I'm saying, "Hang on, let's think that through." For a long time, I thought that made me inconsistent. Now, I see it as harmony – or at least my version of it.

Contradictions are everywhere, not just in people like me. They live in our workplaces too. We see them daily: standards that don't match practices, outdated legislation clashing with modern needs, and policies that seem to contradict the very outcomes they aim to achieve. These inconsistencies can create tension, confusion, and frustration. Yet, if we learn how to navigate them, they also hold the potential for growth, innovation, and a deeper understanding.

We can find harmony in contradiction, challenging the notion that these forces are inherently negative and encouraging a mindset that embraces their coexistence. We often talk about innovation but crave predictability.

We encourage teamwork but celebrate individual success. We want change but get frustrated when things feel uncertain. These mixed messages can feel messy, even uncomfortable, but they're also what keep organisations, and us, alive and learning.

...........................

*I often say contradiction isn't conflict;*
*it's contrast. It's the light and shade that*
*helps us see things more clearly.*

...........................

When we treat every difference as a fight to be won, we miss what that contrast can teach us. The tension isn't the problem; it's the space where new understanding begins. I once coached an Opera Singer – clear proof you don't need to know about the speciality to be able to guide. Ben often applied insights to music; it was his Weird Wisdom. A good piece of music isn't one note on repeat; it's the mix of highs, lows, pauses, and crescendos that make it interesting. Work is like that too. The challenge is to stop trying to iron out every wrinkle and instead ask, *What might this tension be showing me?*

Finding harmony in contradiction doesn't mean everyone has to agree or that we avoid tough conversations. It's about being curious when things feel opposing, and recognising that both sides might hold some truth. Wherever you sit – whether leading a team, part of one, or navigating your day to day – learning to sit in that space between 'this' and 'that' opens new ways of thinking. When we stop seeing contradictions as problems to fix and start seeing them as contrasts to explore, the world doesn't become less complicated, but it does become more interesting, creative, and human.

## REDEFINING CONTRADICTIONS

Contradictions show up every day, often in ways we barely notice. A policy says one thing, but the practice on the ground says another. A team is told to innovate, but the approval process takes 6 months. We talk about work-life balance, while celebrating those who never switch off. These inconsistencies can be frustrating. They can make you question whether anyone actually knows what's going on. But if you look closer, contradictions like these aren't just signs of confusion. They're signs of movement. They show that something is shifting, even if it's messy in the middle.

We tend to see contradictions as problems that need fixing, as if everything should fit neatly into one version of 'right'. But workplaces, like people, are full of competing needs and evolving expectations. Systems built for one time period often have to stretch to fit another. Old habits hang around even when new ideas start taking hold. The frustration you feel when things don't quite line up? That's often the sound of change trying to happen.

Do you recall my initial reluctance to adopt the global definition of 'principles' as fixed, universal truths? If there's one thing I've learnt, it's that accepted truths aren't absolute truths. Absolute truths are rare. Gravity exists. The sun rises in the east. I can remember a time when institutions were heralded as the gold standard in disability care, Pluto was confidently labelled a planet, and the Bay City Rollers were the pinnacle of boy bands. Fast-forward a few decades, and we've revised our understanding of two out of three of those things (and I'll leave it up to you to decide which ones). These examples remind us that truths evolve, shaped by new information, perspectives, and collective experiences.

...............................

*The world is rarely black and white; it thrives
in shades of grey, where contradictions not only
exist but also define the complexity of life.*

...............................

That's what contradictions are — something old and something new coexisting for a while. They show up when our understanding hasn't quite caught up with reality yet. And that's not a flaw in the system; it's a natural part of growth. Contradictions aren't chaos; they're conversation. They show us that learning is still happening.

## FROM POSITION TO PERSPECTIVE

Let's talk about position versus perspective and why this distinction matters wherever you sit in a workplace.

Each of us holds attitudes, values, and beliefs that guide how we live, work, and interact with the world. These are deeply personal, influenced by our upbringing, cultural background, and individual experiences. Given our diverse nature, it's no surprise that our ideas and approaches often conflict. This is particularly evident in workplaces, where teams bring together individuals with varying skills, perspectives, and expectations. These differences can create friction, but they can also be the driving force behind innovation and progress.

Embracing contradictions also involves challenging our own assumptions and biases. Have you ever found yourself holding onto a belief or practice simply because it's familiar or widely accepted? It's human nature to seek comfort in what we know, but this tendency can limit our growth and blind us to new possibilities. By questioning accepted truths and exploring alternative perspectives, we expand our understanding and open ourselves to transformative experiences. This process requires curiosity, courage, and a willingness to embrace discomfort – qualities I believe are essential for personal and professional development.

Position is about being right. It's fixed, defensive, and often shuts down conversation before it even starts. When someone takes a position, the language that comes out is absolute: "You're wrong," "That won't work," "We've always done it this way," or even, "But you just said …" It's no longer about solving a problem or exploring an idea. Instead, they've slid into defending a spot, proving themselves, or protecting their ego. The person speaking from position wants certainty, and they're often unconsciously training everyone else to stop questioning.

Perspective, on the other hand, is about seeing. It's curious, open, and invites dialogue. Perspective-based language sounds very different: "That's interesting, tell me more," "What might we be missing?" "I see it this way, how about you?" It's less about winning and more about understanding. It's the kind of approach that allows tension to coexist with insight and lets different ideas meet without immediate judgement.

The difference isn't subtle. Position closes doors; perspective opens them. Position thrives on certainty; perspective thrives on learning. Position creates friction; perspective creates connection. And yet, workplaces tend to reward position. Think about it – who gets noticed, promoted, or invited into strategic conversations? Usually, the people who speak with confidence, give definitive answers, and appear to have all the solutions. Certainty looks like strength. Position-based thinking might feel effective in the short term, but it often stifles innovation, collaboration, and trust in the long term.

Perspective-taking, on the other hand, is less obviously rewarded. It can look slower, more deliberative, or even less authoritative. But it's the people who ask questions, who pause to see multiple sides, who consider the 'both-and' rather than the 'either-or', who ultimately build teams and cultures that are resilient, adaptable, and creative.

.................................

*Perspective doesn't mean indecision;*
*it means making informed choices with*
*awareness of context, tension, and nuance.*

.................................

Harmony, the kind of harmony that matters in workplaces, comes when we trade the need to be right for the desire to understand. It doesn't mean giving up your voice or never stating your opinion. It means shifting from trying to prove a point to exploring a situation together. It means noticing when your language locks the door and instead choosing words that open it.

When more people in a team or organisation operate from perspective rather than position, something shifts. Conversations become richer. Ideas evolve. People feel heard, valued, and safe to contribute. And, paradoxically, the workplace becomes stronger because it's not being driven by a few fixed opinions, but by the collective insight of its people.

I was observing the business side of a football club during preseason planning. One senior coach, Alex, was known for his cautious and methodical approach. When the club proposed a bold new training regimen designed to boost performance, he raised concerns about player fatigue, injury risk, and reputational damage. The head coach, feeling pressured to agree with the club, pushed for rapid adoption to gain a competitive edge. Early coaching meetings felt like a stand-off.

I noticed that rather than insisting on being 'right', Alex asked curious questions: "What if we trial this with one group first?" and, "How could we monitor workload without slowing progress?" By holding both perspectives – innovation and player safety – he opened the door to constructive progress.

Eventually, the team ran a controlled pilot, or as I like to call it, action-based research, that uncovered early weaknesses, fine-tuned the program, and avoided injuries. Alex's willingness to embrace the tension transformed what could have been conflict into insight. Both caution and ambition were considered, and the team benefited from a stronger, more effective training strategy.

So, wherever you sit, consider this: Is your instinct to be right, or is it to understand? The former wins arguments; the latter wins insight. And insight – that's what moves work, teams, and people forward.

## POSITION VS. PERSPECTIVE: LANGUAGE CHEAT SHEET

**When speaking from position (fixed/right):**
- "You're wrong."
- "That won't work."
- "We've always done it this way."
- "But you just said …"
- "This is the only way."
- "I know best."

**When speaking from perspective (curious/open):**
- "That's interesting, tell me more."
- "What might we be missing?"
- "I see it this way – how about you?"
- "Help me understand your thinking."
- "Here's one possibility, what do you think?"
- "What could we learn from this?"

> ## QUICK TIP
>
> ---
>
> Position closes doors. Perspective opens
> them. Trade the need to be right for the
> desire to understand, and you'll notice that
> conversations shift, as do outcomes.

## THE LANGUAGE OF PARADOX

Our everyday language is full of contradictions, yet we navigate them effortlessly. Take contronyms, words that contain opposing meanings depending on context. To 'dust' can mean to remove particles, like cleaning a shelf, or to sprinkle them, like dusting a cake with sugar. To 'bolt' can mean to secure something firmly or to run away in a rush. To 'sanction' can mean to approve an action or to punish it. These words coexist without causing us confusion; we understand their meaning from context.

| WORD | DEFINITION |
| --- | --- |
| Consult | Offer advice **or** obtain it |
| With | Alongside **or** against |
| Oversight | Monitoring **or** failure to oversee |
| Throw out | Dispose of **or** present for consideration |
| Finished | Completed **or** destroyed |
| Tool | Something useful **or** someone who is not |

If our minds can hold these linguistic contradictions comfortably, why do we struggle so much with contradictions in ideas, perspectives, or people? The answer often lies in our approach to conversation and decision-making. When we speak from a position or a fixed need to be right, we shut down dialogue. Phrases like, "You're wrong," "That won't work" or, "We've always done it this way" signal that the conversation is closed and the other perspective is invalid. In contrast, speaking from perspective invites curiosity. "That's interesting, tell me more" or, "What might we be missing?" encourages exploration, learning, and connection.

Language shapes thinking. When we default to position-based statements, we reinforce rigid thinking, defend past choices, and often resist change. By contrast, perspective-based language nudges us to notice differences, consider alternatives, and embrace ambiguity. It shifts the focus from being right to understanding. In the workplace, this can transform how teams interact: meetings become spaces for curiosity instead of debate; brainstorming sessions open up instead of shutting down, and feedback becomes a tool for insight rather than a weapon.

The cheat sheet of position vs. perspective phrases is more than a linguistic guide. It's a mindset tool. Each time we choose words that open doors and conversation, we're signalling that contradictions aren't threats but opportunities. We're practising the idea that tension can coexist with collaboration, opposing forces don't need resolution to be productive, and harmony doesn't mean sameness.

........................................

*Ultimately, the words we choose can either*
*harden our positions or open our perspectives.*

........................................

Just as our language allows contronyms to exist comfortably, our thinking and our workplaces can learn to hold contradictions without fear. By speaking with curiosity instead of certainty, we create room for dialogue, learning, and innovation. And the more we do it, the more natural it becomes to see difference not as conflict, but as contrast, a space where new possibilities live.

## CONTRADICTION IN PRACTICE: HOLDING THE 'AND'

Work isn't neat. Systems tug one way; people pull another, and priorities constantly collide. You might feel like something has to give – but what if it doesn't? What if you can hold each contradiction lightly? That's the essence of paradox in practice: the 'and', not the 'or'.

Take stability and change. Imagine your team rolling out a new process while keeping core operations running. Stability gives a foundation – you know what works; you know your limits – but change brings growth. One client project may follow a tried-and-true method, while another experiment may test fresh approaches. By holding both, teams avoid chaos without losing opportunity. Reliability anchors the work; adaptability propels it forward.

Or consider individual autonomy and collective responsibility. You want freedom to explore ideas, to experiment, to follow your own instincts. But your team depends on shared outcomes. When both exist, creativity thrives without undermining cohesion. For example, a colleague may test a new campaign approach while checking in with others to ensure alignment.

......................................

*Freedom works because trust is present; responsibility works because everyone understands the bigger picture. Together, they produce results that neither could achieve alone.*

......................................

Confidence and humility in leadership is another classic tension. Strong leaders inspire trust and direction, yet the best also admit when they don't have all the answers. I've seen managers pitch bold strategies to stakeholders while saying to their team, "I want to know what I'm missing here." That combination – boldness tempered by openness – builds respect and invites collaboration. Confidence sets the course; humility keeps eyes and ears open for insight.

Organisations can intentionally hold contradictions too. Healthy workplaces don't just tolerate tension; they embrace it. Cultures that value debate without division and allow rules to be both structure and guideline create space for innovation and accountability. Teams can experiment boldly while still having clear boundaries. Flexible structures evolve with changing demands, while stable foundations ground people. In practice, this means projects are iterative rather than rigid, feedback is ongoing rather than punitive, and everyone knows that challenging ideas isn't a threat – it's welcomed and expected.

When a workplace holds both ideas, tension becomes productive. It sparks creativity, strengthens collaboration, and builds resilience. People feel safe to take risks, to test new approaches, to stretch themselves, and still know they have a solid base to fall back on. Rules and expectations guide without constraining; autonomy exists alongside shared responsibility, and leadership balances decisiveness with listening.

Opposing forces aren't enemies; they're partners.

Stability and change. Freedom and accountability. Confidence and humility. When you stop asking which side 'wins' and start asking how they can coexist, you unlock growth – for you, your team, and your whole organisation. The power is in the 'and'.

## THE ART OF HARMONY

This principle feels like home. It celebrates the messiness, the unpredictability and the realness of being human. Life and work aren't tidy. We have competing desires, conflicting responsibilities, and ideas that push against each other. And that's okay.

Contradictions aren't problems to fix; they're invitations to learn. When you notice tension between caution and courage, freedom and accountability, or confidence and humility, pause and explore it. What can each side teach you? How might both be true at once? The goal isn't resolution in the sense of picking one side, but understanding in the sense of seeing the full picture.

If we can accept the contradictions within ourselves, we open the door to harmony with others. We see that people aren't always simple or predictable and their complexity can be a strength rather than a threat. Work becomes more collaborative, creative, and resilient when we approach it with this mindset.

## IDEAS TO SIT WITH

1. **Contradiction isn't conflict; it's contrast.** Tension isn't the enemy; it's your cue to notice, explore, and learn.
2. **Perspective beats position.** Curious questions open doors; needing to be 'right' shuts them.
3. **It's all about the 'and'.** Stability *and* change. Freedom *and* responsibility. Confidence *and* humility. They all work best together.
4. **Words matter.** The way you speak shapes how you think and how others show up.
5. **Own your contradictions.** The more you accept your own mix of tensions, the easier it is to navigate and celebrate the complexity in others.

# WHAT IF ...?
## (PRINCIPLE FOUR)

## QUESTIONING THE NORMS

Have you noticed how easy it is to fall into the rhythm of *this is how we do things*, with life, work, and even the way we think? So much of it is built on invisible assumptions we hardly question. And that's fine … until it isn't. Because when you stop asking questions, you stop discovering. You stop creating. You stop growing.

Questioning the norms is one of the most powerful things you can do. Not in a disruptive, rebellious way, but in a curious, freeing way. It's about embracing your inner toddler, the one who asks "why?" over and over. Not for the sake of being annoying, but because every *why* is a doorway to understanding, to insight, to something new.

Now, imagine if you questioned even the small things. What if new employees weren't paired with the most experienced staff, but with someone just a few steps ahead of them, someone who's recently navigated the same journey? Suddenly, learning feels relatable. Exploration becomes collaborative. Ideas start flowing in ways we didn't expect.

.......................................

*Ask questions, challenge assumptions, embrace pushback. Resistance isn't a roadblock; it's a sign you're onto something important.*

.......................................

"Yes, but ..." isn't a stop sign; it's an invitation to dig deeper, to see what's really at play.

And let's not forget diversity of thought. When different perspectives collide – engineers, designers, marketers, customer service agents – it can feel messy. But that's where new solutions emerge, ideas flourish, and everyone feels their voice matters. It's not about arguing; it's about exploring, connecting dots, and uncovering possibilities that would have been invisible otherwise.

## THE COMFORT OF CONFORMITY

It's easy to see why we default to conformity. From the moment we're born, we're conditioned to fit in. As children, we're rewarded for following rules, staying in line, and saying the 'right' thing. Society teaches us, subtly and not so subtly, that deviation carries risk.

Being different might mean being ignored, corrected, or even punished. And in a world that often feels uncertain, conformity can feel like a safe harbour, a way to stay visible, valued, and, importantly, unscathed.

Think about work for a moment. You hire for diversity and celebrate different backgrounds, but then you inadvertently ask everyone to fit the same mould. Onboarding and induction, while helpful, often signal what's 'acceptable' and what's not. Over time, those subtle cues smooth out the very differences that made your new hire dynamic in the first place. Their inner Weird Wisdom – their unique perspectives, ideas, and experiences – get muted without you noticing. That's the subtle trap of conformity: it feels safe; it feels easy, but it stifles the very creativity and innovation you're trying to nurture.

And yet, the tension between stability and freedom is exactly what drives innovation. Stability – the predictable systems, the clear processes, the tried-and-true methods – gives people a sense of order. It's essential. Without it, chaos takes over, and teams struggle to move forward. But too much stability? That's where conformity becomes a cage.

...........................

*Innovation demands freedom, the space to explore,
experiment, fail, and try again. It's the discomfort
of uncertainty that births new ideas, and it's in
those moments of tension, when the old and the
new collide, that real breakthroughs happen.*

...........................

This is why understanding the comfort of conformity is so critical. It's not about rejecting rules, structure, or guidance. It's about recognising how easily you slip into the predictable path, how subtle the nudges towards the same shade of beige can be, and how that affects the richness of thought and experience around us. The challenge isn't in creating order. It's in holding space for both order and experimentation at the same time. It's about intentionally asking, *Where am I overvaluing predictability at the expense of creativity? Where are our systems unintentionally silencing ideas?*

So, the next time you notice yourself, or your team, settling into the comfort of conformity, pause. Ask, *Am I following because it works, or because it's safe? Am I preserving order, or am I missing the chance to explore something extraordinary?* The answers can guide not just what you do, but how you think about your team, your culture, and the possibilities waiting just beyond the predictable path.

## THE POWER OF QUESTIONING

There's a real power in questioning. An almost rebellious kind of freedom that doesn't shout or stomp, but quietly opens doors. When you start to explore the assumptions you've been carrying around — those invisible rules that shape how you think, act, and even judge yourself – you create mental space. Space to see things differently, space to imagine alternatives, space to try things that, until now, you assumed were impossible.

. . . . . . . . . . . . . . . . . . . . . . . . . . .

*Questioning is the first step towards*
*liberation. It's a way of telling the world,*
*and yourself, that what you've always been*
*told isn't necessarily the final word.*

. . . . . . . . . . . . . . . . . . . . . . . . . . .

Think back to those 'accepted truths' we explored in previous chapters: the institutions once hailed as gold standards in care, Pluto's planetary status, even the Bay City Rollers at the peak of their boy band fame. We didn't question those truths enough, or we took them for granted. But over time, our understanding evolved. What was once unquestionable shifted, proving that nothing is absolute. By revisiting and questioning assumptions, you give yourself permission to evolve, to adapt, and to see possibilities that were previously invisible. Questioning isn't just a mental exercise; it's a way to reclaim agency over your own thinking.

And here's where your inner toddler comes in. That small, insistent voice inside that asks "why?" relentlessly. Toddlers ask questions because it's how they learn, how they navigate the world, how they make sense of complexity. You've spent years teaching yourself to quiet that voice, to accept the world as it is. But by reconnecting with it, by leaning into that curiosity, you can uncover insights, challenge stale practices, and shake up the status quo. Not for chaos, but for clarity and growth.

In the workplace, questioning norms takes shape in practical, actionable ways. Think again about how you usually buddy up new staff. The assumption is that pairing them with the most experienced employee will help them learn faster. But what if you flipped that? Pairing a new hire with someone 'just in front' on the learning curve creates a different kind of mentoring – one where exploration is shared, mistakes are normal, and problem-solving is a collaborative adventure. Instead of copying the expert, the new hire experiments, asks questions, and discovers solutions in real time, while the 'mentor' is learning alongside them.

This approach also strengthens critical thinking. We learn to analyse information, evaluate perspectives, and consider multiple angles. Linear thinking, where we follow a single path from problem to solution, is replaced with curiosity-driven exploration. You start seeing complexity not as a barrier but as an opportunity to uncover richer, more effective answers. Questioning encourages you and others to embrace nuance, to lean into the tension between ideas, and to recognise that the first answer isn't always the best one.

Recently, I came across a LinkedIn post promoting a new e-training for manual handling, designed specifically for the aged care and disability sectors. The claim? Complete the annual safe lifting training in just 8 minutes. My immediate reaction? *Whoa!* But not in a good way. I found myself asking, *How could something so condensed actually work? Who benefits from this – staff, organisations, or just the bottom line? Cost savings are tempting, but what about the safety of the people actually doing the work?*

Curiosity got the better of me, so I looked into the evidence behind online manual handling training. The findings were disheartening. Research published in 2024 suggests that online training alone is insufficient, and even traditional face-to-face sessions haven't significantly reduced injuries.[4]

This got me thinking: What's training really for? Is it simply about compliance, or is it about genuinely keeping people safe? And here's where the language of rules matters. The Australian Privacy Legislation glossary, for example, makes clear that 'must' is imperative, while 'should' reflects best practice, yet it doesn't define best practice.[5] Catherine Palin Brinkworth CSP (certified speaking professional) told me, "Should is someone else's agenda." That stuck with me. I'm not suggesting we throw the baby out with the bathwater. Traditional training, policies, and legislation have value. They set a baseline. But by questioning the norms, asking the hard questions, and exploring alternative approaches, we might create something that actually works – practical, safe, and fit for purpose.

This isn't just about manual handling. It's about questioning norms wherever they appear: safety protocols, business strategies, even personal habits. Best practice should never be blindly accepted; it should be constantly examined. If you dare to ask why, how, and what for, you open space for solutions that genuinely benefit everyone involved.

Ultimately, the power of questioning lies in its ability to create choice. It's a reminder that you don't have to accept assumptions blindly. You can explore, probe, and challenge. You can give your inner toddler permission to ask how? And in doing so, you unlock perspectives that were previously invisible, opening the door to innovation, understanding, and growth. In a world that often rewards conformity, the courage to question is the freedom to think and act differently.

## MANAGING RESISTANCE

Resistance is part of the human experience. Whenever you challenge assumptions, propose new ideas, or question established norms, you're bound to encounter scepticism, pushback, or even fear of the unknown. It's natural. People feel protective of what they know, of the ways they've always done things. And yet, this resistance isn't a roadblock; it's a signal. It tells you that people are engaged, they care, and there are perspectives or concerns you may not have considered.

The key is learning how to use resistance as a tool. When someone responds with, "Yes, but …" it's not a rejection. Think of it as an invitation. That phrase opens a doorway to explore concerns, uncover hidden barriers, and deepen understanding. By asking questions like, "What do you see as the potential risks here?" or, "How might we address that concern together?" you shift the conversation from confrontation to collaboration. You acknowledge the validity of their perspective while keeping the focus on solutions and shared learning.

Gratitude plays a surprisingly powerful role here.

．．．．．．．．．．．．．．．．．．．．．．．．．．

*Viewing resistance as engagement rather than obstruction changes the energy of the interaction. It encourages curiosity, not defensiveness. Instead of brushing off pushback or reacting emotionally, you can say thank you because their questions and concerns reveal blind spots you might have missed.*

．．．．．．．．．．．．．．．．．．．．．．．．．．

Inviting collaboration requires a gentle, intentional approach. Open-ended questions, reflective listening, and validating different viewpoints create a space where people feel heard rather than attacked. Framing challenges as opportunities for co-creation, rather than as problems to be solved unilaterally, encourages dialogue. The goal isn't to eliminate resistance; it's to transform it into a catalyst for deeper thinking, better solutions, and stronger connections.

In essence, resistance isn't something to fear. It's a conversation starter. Managed with curiosity, gratitude, and collaborative intent, it becomes a springboard for growth.

# INQUIRY VS. INTERROGATION

Asking questions is one of the most powerful tools you have, but it's also one of the easiest to get wrong. I could fill this book with examples of me getting it wrong. What I learnt the hard way is there's a world of difference between inquiry and interrogation. Inquiry comes from curiosity, a desire to understand, explore, and learn. Interrogation comes from judgement, assumption, or the need to defend a position. One opens doors. The other slams them shut.

Effective questioning starts with the language you use. Phrases like, "How did you approach this?" or, "What led you to that decision?" invite reflection. They give people the space to share their thinking without feeling accused. Contrast that with, "Why did you do that?" which, even if asked politely, can trigger defensiveness because it implies there was a mistake. The way you frame your questions either creates insight or fuels resistance. It's subtle, but it matters.

Creating spaces for inquiry is essential, especially when questioning norms or challenging established ways of working. Respect for experience, structure, and context doesn't need to be compromised to encourage open dialogue. People are far more likely to share ideas, explore alternative perspectives, and challenge assumptions when they feel their thoughts are valued, not judged. This is where curiosity and respect intersect, allowing innovation to flourish without tearing down the systems that provide stability.

Encouraging reflection rather than defensiveness is a mindset as much as a skill. Ask yourself: *Do my questions invite exploration, or do they demand justification? Do they uncover possibilities, or highlight failure?*

. . . . . . . . . . . . . . . . . . . . . . . . . . . .

*A simple shift in approach can turn every conversation into an opportunity for shared learning.*

. . . . . . . . . . . . . . . . . . . . . . . . . . . .

Reflection prompts are helpful here. Try pausing and asking yourself, *How can my questions create insight instead of defensiveness?* or, *Am I seeking understanding, or am I seeking validation of my own perspective?* By thinking intentionally about your questions, you model the kind of curiosity you want to see in others.

Inquiry isn't just a communication tool. Think of it as a culture-building tool. When used thoughtfully, it strengthens relationships and opens the door for ideas that may never have emerged in an environment of defensiveness. Curiosity, framed with respect, becomes a bridge to innovation and collaboration.

Ultimately, inquiry is about connection, not confrontation. It's about creating a space where people explore ideas, share perspectives, and challenge assumptions without fear of judgement. When we lead with curiosity, we invite others to do the same, turning questions into opportunities for learning rather than defensiveness. Every conversation becomes a chance to uncover new insights, to see problems from fresh angles, and to discover solutions that might have been hidden behind assumptions or unspoken rules.

Every time you ask thoughtfully, you reclaim choice over assumptions. Every time you shift 'why' to 'how', you invite exploration over defence. By questioning norms, leaning into tension, and embracing curiosity, you unlock growth for yourself and your team. Your questions are the bridge between where you are and true impact begins.

# IDEAS TO SIT WITH

1. **Notice where you fall into the rhythm of conformity.** Pause and ask yourself: *Am I following this process because it works, or because it's safe?* Consider the subtle nudges – culture fit, unspoken rules, meeting habits – that might be smoothing out your or your team's unique contributions.

2. **Reframe your questions from 'why' to 'how'.** 'Why' often triggers defensiveness. 'How' opens doors. Ask yourself: *How could this be done differently? How might we explore alternatives safely?* Reflect on how small shifts in language can change the outcomes of a conversation or project.

3. **Examine best practice critically.** When policies say 'must', it's imperative. 'Should' is best practice – but whose agenda does it serve? As Catherine reminds us, "Should is someone else's agenda." Ask, *Which rules truly serve safety,*

creativity, or impact — and which are just habits we've inherited?

4. **Lean into resistance.** Notice your own pushback or discomfort. Ask, *What's this resistance telling me? How could it guide exploration rather than block it?* Use "Yes, but …" moments as invitations to see hidden barriers or opportunities instead of threats.

5. **Create space for curiosity and connection.** Reflect on your inner toddler – the voice that asks incessantly. Ask, *How can I give myself permission to explore, experiment, and challenge assumptions without creating chaos? How can I model curiosity so others feel safe to do the same?*

# DARE TO DEVIATE
## (PRINCIPLE FIVE)

## CULTURE OR CULT?

Let's start with a question that might make you a little uncomfortable:

**Do you have a culture – or a cult?**

It sounds dramatic, but stay with me. Many organisations proudly celebrate their "positive culture." It's on their websites, in their values posters, and in every second sentence of their job ads. But here's an uncomfortable truth: the line between culture and cult is thinner than most leaders want to admit.

A *culture* builds belonging through respect, curiosity, and individuality. A *cult* builds belonging through control, conformity, and charisma.

A culture celebrates difference. A cult punishes it.

A culture encourages questions. A cult silences them.

A culture thrives on Weird Wisdom. A cult fears it.

Cults don't show up wearing cloaks and chanting in the boardroom. They're subtle. They appear in workplaces that prize harmony over honesty, where questioning leadership is seen as disloyal, and where "we're a family" quietly translates to "don't rock the boat." They thrive when alignment becomes obedience and feedback dries up. What looks like commitment on the surface can, under pressure, reveal itself as control.

So how can you tell the difference? Let's do a quick Weird Wisdom gut check.

## Red Flags – Culture or Cult?

- *Charisma becomes control.* One leader's voice drowns out everyone else's.
- *Belonging costs independence.* You fit in only if you think the same.
- *"We're a family."* Questioning feels like betrayal.
- *No room for dissent.* Silence is safer than speaking
- *Us vs. Them.* Outsiders are dismissed; superiority reinforced.
- *Rituals without reason.* Traditions continue for compliance, not purpose.
- *Loyalty comes at a cost.* Whether emotional or financial, it's transactional, not trust-based.
- Now for the green flags.

## Green Flags – Culture with Weird Wisdom

- *Leaders share the stage.* Influence is earned, not imposed.
- *Individual quirks are assets.* People bring their whole Weird to work.

- *Challenge is welcome.* Dissent sharpens ideas instead of threatening authority.
- *Belonging without conformity.* You fit in because of your difference, not despite it.
- *Open to outside perspectives.* Fresh ideas are invited in, not shut out.
- *Rituals have purpose.* They connect and inspire, not control.
- *Giving outweighs taking.* Energy, ideas, and credit are shared generously.

A culture that fears difference, suppresses questioning, and demands compliance isn't strong. It's fragile. It only survives when everyone agrees not to see the cracks. Weird Wisdom flips that. It thrives on curiosity, honesty, and the courage to ask uncomfortable questions. It gives people permission to notice what isn't working and explore new ways. Even when – no, *especially when* – it's awkward, messy, or slow.

That's why *exploring the unconventional* matters so much. It's the antidote to conformity disguised as unity. It's what keeps culture from tipping into cult.

Exploring the unconventional isn't about clichés, thinking outside the box, or ignoring the rules. Those rules, policies, standards, and ethics? They're boxes, and they're not going away. They're not there to trip you up. They're your tools. And if you embrace them as such, Weird Wisdom works beautifully, even in compliance-heavy industries like healthcare, aged care, and finance. But honestly, it works anywhere people are willing to play with perspective.

Exploring the unconventional is a mindset. It's curiosity wrapped in courage. It's noticing the hidden possibilities inside constraints. It's asking, "Why have we always done it this way?" and, "How could this work differently?" without thinking you need to dismantle everything.

. . . . . . . . . . . . . . . . . . . . . . . . . . . . .

*Weird Wisdom thrives when you value perspectives others might call Weird, offbeat, or unconventional. Those are the ideas conventional thinking misses, and often they're the ones that create breakthroughs.*

. . . . . . . . . . . . . . . . . . . . . . . . . . . . .

Imagine a nurse spotting a safer workflow, an educator finding a more engaging lesson, or a marketer dreaming up a campaign nobody else would dare try. None of this happens by accident. It happens because rules became tools, not brick walls. Because curiosity was encouraged, not shut down. Because Weird Wisdom was allowed to shine.

And it doesn't stop at compliance-heavy industries. When unconventional thinking is welcomed, business, community, education, anywhere people work together benefits. By seeing rules as guides rather than cages, you create space for experimentation, innovation, and ideas that actually improve outcomes.

So next time a policy, procedure, or standard crosses your path, don't groan. Pause. Ask, "How can this help us do something different?" Weird Wisdom isn't about breaking rules; it's about using what you've got to make work, people, and outcomes better.

## THE POWER OF WEIRD WISDOM

The power of diverse perspectives is often underestimated. When we truly value all voices, not just the loudest or the highest-ranking, something remarkable happens: people engage more, contribute more, and innovate more. Diverse perspectives aren't just about leadership or seniority; they come from everywhere in the workplace. From administration staff to frontline teams, from interns to long-tenured specialists, every experience, insight, and viewpoint has the potential to unlock ideas that wouldn't otherwise surface.

One of the sneakiest traps in any organisation is groupthink. It doesn't only show up in the boardroom or the executive suite; it thrives anywhere you're only listening to one group. It could be a team that's been in the same sector for decades, staff who've only ever worked for one employer, or a department that's always done things "this way." None of these experiences are wrong. But if they're the only voices heard, innovation stalls. Ideas narrow, creativity shrinks, and adaptability suffers. Blind spots emerge, particularly around culture, inclusion, and strategy, because the lens is limited.

The antidote? Actively seek a range of voices. Encourage dialogue across levels, roles, and experiences. Ask questions like, "How would you approach this if you were in a completely different department?" or, "What have you seen elsewhere that might work here?" Listen, not just to reply, but to understand. How's that for a cliché? Weird

Wisdom flourishes when curiosity guides conversation and assumptions are challenged.

Collaboration amplifies this effect. When people with different experiences – operations, customer service, marketing, finance, and beyond – work together, they start connecting dots that weren't even visible before. The energy moves from defending familiar approaches to exploring possibilities. Motivation rises because people feel their ideas matter. Engagement grows because they see their perspectives shaping outcomes. Innovation emerges naturally, driven by the collision of unique experiences and creative thinking.

Diverse perspectives also safeguard organisations against stagnation. They create flexibility to adapt when environments change, help uncover hidden risks, and foster a culture where dissent isn't punished but valued. When people feel safe to challenge the status quo, you see solutions emerge that a single perspective would never have spotted.

In the end, embracing diverse perspectives isn't just a nice-to-have. In my opinion, it's essential. It's about recognising that no single group, role, or experience has a monopoly on Wisdom.

*Weird Wisdom shows us that the richest insights come when every voice has space, every story is heard, and curiosity is welcomed.*

That's how engagement, innovation, and growth really take off.

## OVERCOMING INERTIA

Inertia can be tricky. It sneaks in both when we struggle to start something new and when we can't seem to stop doing things that no longer serve us. It's those long-standing habits, entrenched processes, and familiar ways of working that feel safe, comfortable, and fuel the mindset of "that's just how we do things." And yet, over time, they quietly hold us back from innovation, efficiency, and growth. Recognising inertia isn't about blaming anyone or pointing fingers; it's about noticing where the old ways are running on autopilot and asking whether they still meet the needs of your team, your organisation, and the people you serve.

Engaging with this inertia means being curious about what's happening beneath the surface. Which practices are outdated? Which workflows create unnecessary friction? And importantly, whose voices haven't been heard in assessing these routines? It's easy to assume that the people in leadership or long-tenured staff hold all the answers, but innovation often comes from unexpected places. Those who experience processes day to day, those with diverse experiences across sectors, or even someone new who sees things with fresh eyes. By intentionally seeking these perspectives, you create opportunities to challenge assumptions and rethink what 'normal' looks like.

The first step is to recognise the habits that no longer serve your organisation. Take a look around. Are there workflows that feel unnecessarily complicated? Practices that take up more time than they should? Meetings that happen because "we've always had them" rather than because they add value? None of this is unusual. Every organisation has areas where the routine has outlasted its usefulness. Identifying them is the first step to creating space for something better.

Once you know what's no longer working, it's time to engage a diverse group of people for fresh perspectives.

And when I say diverse, I mean across the whole organisation. Not just leadership, not just your department, not just those you agree with. Frontline staff, administration, new hires, long-tenured employees. Everyone sees and experiences the system differently. Their Weird Wisdom, their unique experiences and insights can reveal opportunities you might never have noticed.

Now, here's where mindset comes into play. Too often, rules, policies, and compliance criteria are seen as stop signs. But they're actually the boundaries that define the playing field. Within those boundaries, you can explore, experiment, and innovate. Ask yourself, *How can we meet this requirement in a new or more effective way?* That question alone shifts your thinking from doing the bare minimum to finding solutions that add real value.

Imagine you have a compliance requirement that certain workflows must be documented, checked, and approved in a set sequence. The conventional approach is to follow the steps exactly as prescribed. But by stepping back, looking at the purpose of the rule, and inviting fresh perspectives, you might redesign the workflow to be simpler, faster, and less error-prone, while still meeting every compliance requirement. Or consider a process that requires multiple approvals from different departments. Could you redesign it so approvals happen in parallel rather than in sequence? The rule hasn't changed, but your approach has become more effective.

Being unconventional isn't about creating chaos; it's about calculated exploration within boundaries. It's about curiosity, critical thinking, and the willingness to ask "why?" "how?" and "what if?" It's about allowing ideas to be tested, refined, and improved without fear of failure. And yes, failure might happen. But each misstep is data, an insight, a chance to get closer to something that actually works.

The beauty of this approach is it scales. From compliance-heavy industries like healthcare and finance to creative, fast-moving sectors, the principles are the same: identify what's not working, challenge assumptions, invite diverse perspectives, and reimagine processes. Not for the sake of change, but for better outcomes, safer practices, and a more engaged workforce.

Overcoming inertia isn't about tearing everything down or breaking the rules. It's about shifting perspective. It's about recognising that the routines you inherited aren't sacred; they're starting points.

...........................

*With curiosity, critical thinking, and the collective Weird Wisdom of your people, you can turn stagnation into momentum, friction into flow, and old habits into new opportunities.*

...........................

So, the next time you catch yourself doing something because "that's how it's always been done," pause. Ask, explore, experiment. Within the boundaries that define your field, there's an entire world of possibility waiting for your Weird Wisdom to bring it to life.

## CREATING OPPORTUNITIES

Whose perspective are you missing right now? Think about it. Too often, we fall into the habit of listening only to the usual voices, the ones we expect, the ones who fit in. But the most valuable insights, the ones that spark real change, often come from unexpected places. They come from those quick hallway conversations, the side discussions after a team meeting, or that spontaneous 5-minute problem-solving chat. These are the moments where ideas hide, waiting for someone, maybe you, to notice them.

Please don't be tempted to rely solely on suggestion boxes or annual surveys to uncover those ideas. They have their place, but they're static. They wait for feedback instead of inviting it in real time. If you want to tap into your team's Weird Wisdom, you need to create space for curiosity, experimentation, and questions. Ask yourself, and others, "Why have we always done it this way?" Notice the routines and processes that happen because that's just the way they've always been done. Sometimes the most powerful insights come not from what you add, but from what you choose not to do.

Look around your workplace. Are departments talking only to themselves? Marketing knows what works for clients; operations knows the workflows inside out, and customer service experiences the challenges first-hand. If these teams never collaborate, their knowledge stays isolated. But when you bring them together to explore solutions, things change. Suddenly, connections emerge that nobody saw alone. Ideas flow. Problems get solved faster. And yes, you start seeing the Weird Wisdom everyone brings to the table.

You don't have to be the CEO or a manager to create

this culture. You can spark curiosity, ask the hard questions, and challenge assumptions no matter your role. That moment when you ask, "What if we tried this differently?" might be small, but it's contagious. Others start thinking the same way. Others start experimenting. And that's how a culture of Weird Wisdom grows.

Think about your own experiences. When was the last time someone really listened to your unconventional idea and acted on it? Felt safe to take a calculated risk? Felt that their unique perspective mattered? That's what we're talking about here. That's what you can create around you, right now.

Real collaboration isn't just about getting people in a room. It's about listening, reflecting, and resisting the urge to respond with a quick, "Yes, but …"

*The new ideas are usually the uncomfortable ones. The ones that challenge the status quo. Your job, and mine, is to hold space for those ideas, test them, learn from them, and then share what works with others.*

So, I want you to notice the opportunities around you – the overlooked voices, the small gaps in your day, the what ifs waiting to be asked. Embrace curiosity, encourage cross-team collaboration, and value perspectives from every level of your workplace. Do this, and you're not just solving problems; you're creating a culture where Weird Wisdom thrives, where people feel seen, heard, and motivated to shape something extraordinary with you.

## MANAGING RESISTANCE

Exploring the unconventional isn't always about grand invention. Often, it's about finally noticing what's been sitting right under your nose. But when we've done something the same way for too long, our blinkers stop us from seeing what's possible.

I once worked for a statewide community services organisation. Small state, big organisation. In my area, I was the odd one out. I'd worked in other parts of community services, for different organisations, across different states, and in a variety of roles. Everyone else had only ever worked in this organisation, in this same business area. That didn't make them wrong and me right, but it did mean that groupthink was alive and well – and I was the Weird one. You know, the one asking questions. The one gently prodding exploration of the unconventional. The one asking, "What if …?" while everyone else just wished I'd stop rocking the boat. And to be fair, from their perspective, it probably felt that way.

The issue at hand was the on-call procedure, specifically, how staff were rostered. The system was causing real distress. People were getting so many calls they couldn't have a shower, feed their kids, or get enough sleep. When I suggested we explore other ways to manage it, the shutters came down fast. The senior leader didn't want to know.

Eventually, at a meeting I wasn't part of, it was decided to send out a staff survey to gauge how people were feeling. When the results came in, the responses were brutally honest – the on-call staff had named exactly what was broken. Instead of being curious, the leaders were disappointed and defensive. They didn't want to share the results or talk about them.

We were due for a quarterly all-in meeting, and I asked for on-call to be added to the agenda. The day came, and the mood in the room was … let's just say 'professionally tense'. The leadership team clearly didn't want change. I threw out a few ideas for discussion, only to be met with, "No, that won't work" and my personal favourite, "Don't try bringing other states' ways here."

I was running out of road. The on-call team was burnt out, and I was out of ideas. So, I took a deep breath and asked one simple question: "How is the organisation planning to address the mental health concerns raised in the survey?"

That word 'how' changed everything. Not because it magically solved the problem, but because it shifted the conversation. 'Why' had been met with defensiveness; 'how' invited responsibility. There was movement – reluctant, messy, half-hearted, but movement all the same.

Did it feel like success? No, not really. The leaders never truly listened to the diverse perspectives of their on-call team, and the 'new system' they built didn't address the real issue. But it was a start.

............................

*Systems and structures exist for a reason, but when they stop serving the people they're meant to help, we have to question them. Not to be difficult, but to create something that actually works.*

............................

That's why Weird Wisdom matters. It's not about being rebellious. It's about seeing the blind spots that others have learnt to ignore. It's about asking better questions, especially the *how* ones, exploring the unconventional, and having the courage to keep asking, even when the room goes quiet.

I could give plenty of examples of me riding in on my white horse and creating some miraculous outcome via exploring the unconventional. You could find heaps of other examples by doing a quick online search. But this book isn't about blowing my own trumpet or proving a point. The example I gave is messy. It's real. In my view, its imperfection makes it the perfect example.

Because progress doesn't always look like a win. Sometimes it's just the first nudge that makes space for the next person to keep asking.

## IDEAS TO SIT WITH

1. **Rules can be tools.** When you see a policy or standard, do you view it as a barrier or a boundary to play within? Try seeing the 'rules' not as constraints that stop you but as tools that support what you can do.

2. **Whose voice is missing?** When was the last time you invited a perspective from outside your usual circle? Innovation doesn't just come from leaders; it comes from anyone who sees things differently. Ask yourself: *Who isn't in this conversation that should be?*

3. **We find comfort in the familiar.** Notice where comfort might be holding you back. What practices, meetings, or habits are still in place simply because "that's how we've always done it"? Inertia isn't always loud – sometimes it's disguised as tradition.

4. **See resistance as engagement.** Next time you get pushback, instead of seeing it

as opposition, ask *how* you can use it. 'How' opens possibilities; 'why' often builds walls. Resistance means people care – use that energy to find a way forward together.

5. **Find Weird Wisdom in everyday moments.** Exploring the unconventional doesn't have to be dramatic. It can start with a hallway chat, a curious question, or a small tweak to a process. Pay attention to the everyday opportunities to apply your Weird Wisdom – that's where real change begins.

# NO MORE WAITING:
## YOUR WEIRD WISDOM STARTS TODAY

## A RALLYING CRY

Weird Wisdom isn't something you file away for later. It begins with you, today. It doesn't wait for the perfect role, the right title, or a formal mandate. You don't need policies, budgets, or committees to act. The spark starts with the choices you make in this moment: noticing an idea, speaking up, pausing to see what others might miss. These are the small acts where Weird Wisdom takes root.

Personal agency is at the heart of Weird Wisdom. Every experience, insight, and perspective shaped by your life, no matter how ordinary it seems, carries value. Your Weird Wisdom is uniquely yours, and it has the power to influence others, kickstart ideas, and change how work gets done.

But Weird Wisdom isn't just about you. It's also about the people around you, the colleagues whose ideas are half-formed, whose contributions are overlooked, or whose voices are hesitant in meetings. Supporting them doesn't require a leadership title. Noticing, listening, and creating space for others to step into their own Weird Wisdom is powerful. Sometimes it's a simple question: "That's an interesting thought, can you tell me more?" Other times it's acknowledging a different perspective when it's being ignored, or quietly ensuring someone's insight is seen before it's dismissed.

Every time you embrace your Weird Wisdom and make room for others, a ripple begins. Teams become more collaborative; ideas flow more freely, and people take risks they might otherwise avoid. The workplace becomes richer, not just in outcomes, but in how people feel seen, respected, and valued. No policies, budgets, or decrees are needed, just the acts of noticing, supporting, and acting.

## REVISITING THE MYTHS – THE FIVE PRINCIPLES RECAP

### 1. Getting Comfortable with the Unknowns

Uncertainty isn't a pathway to fear; it's a playground for creativity. When clarity isn't perfect, opportunities appear. Experimenting, testing, and exploring the unknown stretches us and sparks new perspectives.

### 2. Embracing Failure as Growth

Failure isn't a verdict; it's data. Each misstep carries lessons if we lean in, analyse, and apply them. Mistakes become tools for learning, not threats to competence.

## 3. Finding Harmony in Contradictions

Conflicting ideas aren't problems; they're opportunities. Contradictions encourage curiosity, deeper thinking, and integration of multiple perspectives. Harmony means valuing differences, not enforcing agreement.

## 4. Questioning the Norms

While assumptions guide work, they can also limit it. Asking, "Is there another way?" creates space for improvement, efficiency, and fresh solutions.

## 5. Exploring the Unconventional

Thinking differently sparks real change. Challenging routines and assumptions opens doors to innovation. Small experiments with unconventional ideas often yield solutions that standard approaches miss.

...............................

*Weird Wisdom doesn't depend on hierarchy, titles, or authority. It exists in every role, experience, and perspective. By embracing your own and noticing it in others, you create a ripple of curiosity, courage, and collaboration.*

...............................

## OWN IT – YOUR WEIRD WISDOM MATTERS

Every person carries unique experiences and insights, even when working in similar roles. Ask yourself: *What's unique about my perspective?* As I said in the introduction, Weird Wisdom isn't something you pick up later in life like a skill. It's something you reconnect with. What *can* be learnt is how to use it effectively. When you embrace your Weird Wisdom, your work improves, and you quietly create space for others to do the same. Influence doesn't come from titles or authority. It comes from showing up authentically, noticing ideas, and taking small, intentional actions. No budget, policy, or permission required.

Common myths:

◆ "I need authority to make a difference." Influence starts with showing up.

◆ "Everyone thinks the same. I can't contribute." Your lived experience is unique.

◆ "Change needs money, policies, or a plan." Action starts with curiosity and courage.

## SMALL ACTIONS, BIG IMPACT

1. **Share early, share often.** Offer a half-formed idea to spark conversation.

2. **Notice and validate others.** Recognise perspectives: "I hadn't thought of it that way, thanks for sharing."

3. **Lead differently.** Speak last, restructure discussions, create space for quieter voices.

4. **Ask curious questions.** Challenge assumptions without judgement: "What if we looked at this differently?"

5. **Experiment boldly.** Try low-risk ideas, observe, adjust, and share learnings.
6. **Support ideas under threat.** Validate or advocate for overlooked contributions.
7. **Make it daily.** Use every conversation to encourage curiosity, share insights, and celebrate Weird Wisdom.

An organisation in Perth called me after their engagement survey. On the surface, results looked decent – better-than-average response rates and the usual minor issues – but the CEO and chairman were worried about tension between departments. We agreed to focus on their two highest-priority areas and got to work. Nine months later, I returned onsite. The staff who had undergone training and coaching were interacting differently – messily, imperfectly, but genuinely trying. While I'd trained the staff, I hadn't trained the executives, and I didn't know how to raise the subject.

During our onsite meeting, the CEO slid a report across the table. The results stunned me. Since I'd trained their staff, bullying within the organisation had reduced by a whopping 71.6 percent – and bullying wasn't even one of the two priorities we had set. It hadn't been discussed in planning meetings at all. I asked where the remaining 28 percent was occurring. The chairman smiled: "You're training us next."

The impact was undeniable. Workplace bullying costs millions in lost productivity, turnover, and legal risk, and carries a huge human toll – stress, anxiety, and disengagement. By embracing the five Weird Wisdom principles, this organisation didn't just lift engagement scores; they transformed behaviours, reduced conflict, and boosted morale.

........................................

*Real results happen when people are supported to use their Weird Wisdom. It spreads beyond the original focus areas, creating measurable change in ways no one could have predicted.*

........................................

When you connect your Weird Wisdom with others, incredible things happen. Different perspectives collide and combine, helping you make smarter decisions and see solutions you'd never notice alone. Hidden tensions surface before they spiral, allowing you to fix problems early and keep morale high. Trust grows, respect deepens, and teams become more creative, resilient, and effective. When people feel their unique ideas are seen and valued, change isn't just planned – it sticks!

You don't need a title, a policy, or a committee to start. Small, intentional acts – pausing to hear a quiet voice, asking a curious question, or supporting an idea before it's fully formed – change the way work gets done and how people feel while doing it. Every thoughtful action adds up, making a workplace where contribution, experimentation, and collaboration thrive.

And before you go … what's one thing you can do before lunchtime tomorrow that costs nothing, needs no approval, and lets you step into your Weird Wisdom? Do it. Today.

# ACKNOWLEDGEMENTS

This book belongs to my *Framily*, a slightly strange word for the group that includes family by birth and those friends who, through longevity and heart, are indistinguishable from family. Your quiet confidence in me, the well-timed kicks up the bum, and the constant encouragement to do better and be better have carried me further than you realise. Even if I still suspect some of you were throwing my own sayings back at me.

Within that group, special thanks goes to my sister, Sheelagh. Never the most effusive, but unwavering. She simply says she knows I'll do what I'll do, no matter how out of reach it appears. That steady belief matters more than you know.

And to my twin brother, Ralph: thank you for a

lifetime of practice in holding contradictions lightly. It turns out that was excellent preparation for writing this book. And PS, I don't make excuses for people. lol

To Carmen Braidwood: you thought you were teaching me 'Confidence on Camera' and 'Media Training'. What actually happened was a series of well-timed, slightly inconvenient doorstop questions that forced me to sharpen my thinking, fast. You clarified my ideas on Weird Wisdom far more than planned, and definitely more than advertised.

Then there are the people I've never formally met and yet who somehow co-wrote this book with me anyway. The ones at the gym, on planes, in waiting rooms, at events, and in places I can't even remember. You asked, "So, what do you do?" I answered. You paused, nodded, and said, "You should write a book." At the time, I laughed it off. But hearing it over and over lodged something. This book exists because enough strangers saw something worth naming before I fully did.

To Susan Dean at Dean Publishing, your support and encouragement from our very first conversation made this book possible. You never tried to tame the idea or talk me out of this being the start of a series. When I began writing, I didn't even have a title. It was Senior

Editor Natalie Deane who said, "You're calling it *Weird Wisdom*, aren't you?" She was right.

Thank you also to the wider Dean team. Matt Moore, in particular, for pushing me to include more stories. While I felt a strong internal resistance to these stories sounding like bragging, your instinct was spot on.

To my fellow Dean Author Retreat attendees: we came together for 2 days, all at different stages of our writing journeys. It was that diversity that inspired me to keep going. It also helped me realise this book was drifting dangerously close to thesis territory, weighed down with references, quotes, and proof that Weird Wisdom was 'a thing'. I paused, stripped it back, and trusted the work.

That reset happened in the small Tasmanian town of Westbury, small in size, big in heart. It was there I reclaimed my enthusiasm for this book, helped in no small part by the interest and curiosity of the people I met along the way. Lucy from *Love Lucy Boots* and Sam, "He's a craftsman, not a tradesman," deserve special mention. Thank you for the laughs and the robust conversations while waiting for my long black.

This book is better because of all of you.

# ABOUT THE AUTHOR

Trish Goodfield is one of Australia's leading diversity of thought experts, known for making complex ideas practical and usable in real workplaces.

With more than 4 decades of experience across community services, health, disability, government, and business sectors, Trish has worked at every level of organisations, from frontline roles to executive leadership and boardrooms. That breadth shapes her calm, grounded approach to leadership, performance, and culture.

Most organisations say they value different perspectives. Very few know how to turn them into clear decisions, honest conversations, and consistent results.

Trish's work focuses on closing that gap. She helps leaders, teams, and organisations bring diversity of thought to the forefront, not as a slogan, but as a practical lever for better thinking, better outcomes, and less daily friction.

She is the creator of *Weird Wisdom*®, a framework built on the idea that what's often dismissed as unconventional, uncomfortable, or unclear is frequently the very thing organisations need to pay attention to. Through consulting, facilitation, coaching, and speaking, Trish helps people uncover blind spots, ease tension, and shift the patterns that quietly keep workplaces stuck.

When Trish isn't working, she's still observing how people think, speak, and navigate contradiction – in meetings, airports, cafes, and the everyday spaces where human behaviour tells the real story. You might also find her trackside watching motor racing, drawn to the mix of precision, risk, teamwork, and split-second decision-making. Or crafting, where patience, experimentation, and imperfect outcomes are part of the process. Both worlds feed her work: one loud and fast, the other quiet and deliberate, a reminder that progress rarely comes from choosing one way of being over another, but from learning how to hold both.

You can connect with Trish and
explore her work at:

Web: trishgoodfield.com

Blog: diversityofthought.org

linkedin.com/in/trishgoodfield

# ENDNOTES


1   Oxford Languages (n.d.) 'Weird', accessed 8 December 2025.

2   Findeiss L, Spencer B, and Ray CE Jr (2017) 'Diversity of Thought', Seminars in Interventional Radiology, 34(1):1–2, doi.org/10.1055/s-0036-1597768.

3   Oxford Languages (n.d.) 'Principle', accessed 8 December 2025.

4   Kugler HL, Taylor NF, and Brusco NK (2024) 'Patient Handling Training Interventions and Musculoskeletal Injuries in Healthcare Workers: Systematic Review and Meta-Analysis', Heliyon, 10(3), doi.org/10.1016/j.heliyon.2024.e24937.

5   Office of the Australian Information Commissioner (22 July 2019) 'Chapter A: Introductory Matters', Australian Government, accessed 11 December 2025, https://www.oaic.gov.au/privacy/australian-privacy-principles/australian-privacy-principles-guidelines/chapter-a-introductory-matters.